All Clear! Intro—

Speaking, Listening, Expressions, and Pronunciation in Context

Helen Kalkstein Fragiadakis,

Contra Costa College
San Pablo, California

Heinle & Heinle Publishers
I(T)P An International Thomson Publishing Company

Pacific Grove • Albany • Bonn • Boston • Cincinnati • Detroit • London • Madrid • Melbourne
Mexico City • New York • Paris • San Francisco • Tokyo • Toronto • Washington

The publication of **All Clear Intro** was directed by members of the Newbury House ESL/EFL team at Heinle & Heinle:

Erik Gundersen, Editorial Director
Jonathan Boggs, Market Development Director
Maryellen Eschmann Killeen, Production Services Coordinator
Kristin Thalheimer, Senior Production Services Coordinator
Thomas Healy, Developmental Editor

Also participating in the publication of this program were:

Stanley J. Galek, Vice President and Publisher
Ken Pratt, Associate Editor
Amy Lawler, Managing Developmental Editor
Mary Sutton, Associate Market Development Coordinator
Mary Beth Hennebury, Manufacturing Coordinator
Heide Kaldenbach-Montemayor, Assistant Editor
Rotunda Design: Cover Design
Brian Orr: Illustrator
Margaret Cleveland: Project Manager
Accu-Color, Inc.: Composition
Carol Rose: Interior design

LIBRARY OF CONGRESS CATALOGING-IN-PUBLICATION DATA

Fragiadakis, Helen Kalkstein.
  All Clear! Intro: Speaking, listening, expressions, and pronunciation in context/Helen Kalkstein Fragiadakis
    p. cm.
  Includes index.
  ISBN
  1. English language—Textbooks for foreign speakers. 2. English language—Pronunciation.
3. English language—Idioms. I. Title
PE1128.F63   1997
428.2'4-dc20

96-30941
CIP

Heinle & Heinle Publishers/A Division of International Thomson Publishing, Inc.

Manufactured in the United States of America

ISBN 08384-6030-5

10 9 8 7 6 5 4 3 2

To my family—

All Clear! Intro
A Walk-Through Guide

All Clear! Intro—aimed at high-beginning students, is the first in this best-selling series of conversationally-oriented texts. High-frequency American English expressions such as *hold on a minute,* and *wake up* are presented in meaningful contexts to develop speaking, listening, and pronunciation skills. This text is also appropriate for vocabulary courses.

1. Warm up

- Introduces the topic of each lesson
- Activates students' background knowledge and vocabulary

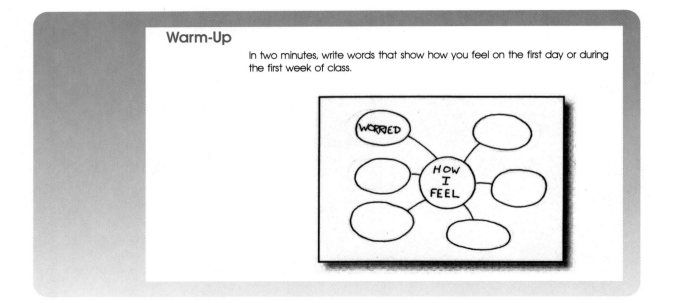

Warm-Up

In two minutes, write words that show how you feel on the first day or during the first week of class.

2. Focused listening

- High-frequency American English expressions are presented in interesting contexts
- Pre-listening, as you listen, and post-listening exercises develop listening skills

Focused Listening

BEFORE YOU LISTEN

- Look at the cartoon on page 1. It is the first day of school. With a partner, answer, this question: What do you think the two students, Andy and Eric, are talking about?

- Read these five sentences. *Don't give the answers now.* These sentences can be true or false (not true). Or, it may not be possible to know if a sentence is true or false.

_____ 1. Eric is worried and shy, and Andy is helping him.

_____ 2. Andy is not nervous.

_____ 3. Eric will make many friends in this class.

_____ 4. The teacher wants students to talk in this class.

_____ 5. Eric and Andy are best friends.

"Author has a *great* sense of what beginning students can handle."

Pianta, *San Diego Mesa College*

3. Dialogue

- Lively, natural language provides the source of pronunciation and speaking activities

uh-huh = yes, uh-uh = no	

ANDY: **What's wrong**, Eric?

ERIC: I'm really nervous. I'm always this way on the first day of school.

ANDY: You're not the only one. It's hard for me, too. I'm glad we're **taking** this **class** together.

ERIC: Do you know anything about the teacher?

ANDY: Uh-huh, a little. Someone told me she gives a lot of homework, and you **have to** talk a lot in class.

ERIC: Oh, no! **I'm afraid of** talking in front of a lot of people.

ANDY: Oh, **don't worry.** Everyone's afraid **at the beginning,** but after you **get to know** the people and **make friends**…

ERIC: It doesn't **get better** for me. I'm shy. I **have trouble** looking at people when I talk, and my hands shake.

ANDY: Look…the teacher's here. Let's talk after class.

4. Understanding the New Expressions

● New expressions are explained in context

● Activities encourage students to produce new language

● Clear examples provide vocabulary support

All Clear?

YES	NO

1. What's wrong?

Note: You ask this question when you see a person with a problem. *Pronunciation Note:* *What* + *is* can become a contraction pronounced as one word: *what's.*

S1: **What's wrong?**
S2: I have a headache.
I feel sick.
My test was hard.
I'm tired.
My car doesn't work.

Similar Expression: **What's wrong with _____?**

S1: **What's wrong with** you? You look tired.
S2: I am tired. I didn't sleep last night.

Your Turn: Think about your friends and family. When do you say, "What's wrong?"

I ask "What's wrong?" when: someone is _____.
                                    someone is _____.

● Self-monitoring activities encourage students to take charge of their own learning

"All the contexts are useful, meaningful and appropriate—and there is ample practice with the expressions."

Victoria Badalamenti, *La Guardia Community College*

5. Exercises

● A variety of exercise types serve different learning styles. Three examples are mentioned below: Whole class surveys, language learning games, and listening activities.

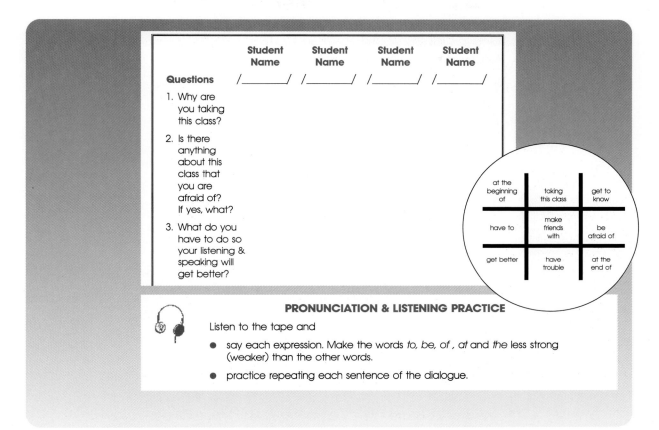

"*All Clear! Intro* offers very comprehensive coverage of speaking, listening, vocabulary and pronunciation…with diverse approaches for visual, auditory, and kinesthetic learners."

Sally Gearhart, *Santa Rosa Junior College*

Contents

Icebreaker   xix

(Expressions in parentheses are explained in the Understanding the Expressions section. They do not appear in the introductory dialogue.)

Lesson 1: What's Wrong?   1

Situation: It is the first day of school, and two friends are talking to each other in class before the teacher enters.

Listening/Speaking Focus: Starting a New Class

Expressions: what's wrong, take __ class, have to, be afraid of, don't worry (worry about), at the beginning, (at the end), get to know, make friends, get better, have trouble

Pronunciation Point: Stress and Reduced Forms "hafta" and "hasta"

Lesson 2: Who's This?   19

Situation: Alex calls Sara on the phone to invite her to the movies.

Listening/Speaking Focus: Making Telephone Invitations

Expressions: who's this, (who's calling), it's. . . , this is. . . , hold on, (answer the phone, get the phone, hang up), it's for you, I'll be right there, can't make it, why don't. . . , pick up, that sounds____, get off

Pronunciation Point: Stress in Two-Word Verbs; Contractions

Review: Crossword Puzzles for Lessons 1 & 2   36

Lesson 3: Let's Go Away for the Weekend   39

Situation: A couple are making plans to go away for a weekend.

Listening/Speaking Focus: Making Plans for the Weekend

Expressions: go away (go on a trip, take a trip), go swimming (go __ing), take walks (take a walk), what else, plenty of, be crowded (a crowd), make a reservation, lots of (a lot of)

Pronunciation Point: Sentence Stress

Lesson 4: Wake Up!   57

Situation: It is very early in the morning, and one roommate is trying to get another roommate to wake up because he has to go to the airport.

Listening/Speaking Focus: Describing Your Daily Routine

Expressions: wake up, (fall asleep), get up, get out of bed, go back to sleep, have a good trip, (take a trip), go to bed, need to, take a shower, (take a bath), have time for (to), get dressed, (get undressed, put on, take off)

Pronunciation Point: Intonation

Review: Crossword Puzzle for Lessons 3 & 4   80

Lesson 5: Are You Ready to Order?   83

Situation: A brother is taking his sister out for lunch for her birthday.

Listening/Speaking Focus: Ordering in a Restaurant

Expressions: once in a while, whatever (wherever/whenever) you want, I'll have, be hungry (be starving, be thirsty), Are you ready to order? (Can I take your order? We're ready to order.), would like (What would you like? Would you like. . . ?), for now, How about you? (And you?), Will that be all? (Is that it?), That's all. (That's it.)

Pronunciation Point: Stress and Intonation

Appendices

Index: Alphabetical List of Expressions 197

Thank You

The author and publisher would like to thank the following individuals who offered many helpful insights during the planning for and development of **All Clear! Intro:**

Heidi Aboutaj, *Texas Wesleyan University*

Victoria Badalamenti, *La Guardia Community College, New York*

Liza Becker, *Mt. San Antonio College, California*

Charles Brown, *Concordia University, Quebec*

Barbara Campbell, *State University of New York at Buffalo*

Sally Gearhart, *Santa Rosa Junior College, California*

Steve Horowitz, *Central Washington University*

Patricia McGee, *Camden County College, New Jersey*

Gregory O'Dowd, *Tokai University, Japan*

Pianta, *San Diego Mesa College, California*

Germaine Tilney, *Florida International University*

Jilani Warsi, *Newbury College, Massachusetts*

Acknowledgments

Thank-you to Heinle & Heinle for giving me this opportunity to complete the *All Clear* series with this introductory text. A very special thank-you goes to my Developmental Editor, Thomas Healy, who was always supportive, insightful, thorough, and a great pleasure to work with.

To Charles Heinle, President; Stan Galek, Vice President and Publisher; and John McHugh, National Field Sales Manager, I send my appreciation.

Thank-you to Erik Gundersen for your guidance early on and throughout in this project, and to Dr. June McKay for your absolutely invaluable feedback and support.

At Heinle & Heinle, I'd also like to thank Kristin Thalheimer, Senior Production Services Coordinator; Maryellen Eschmann Killeen, Production Services Coordinator; Jonathan Boggs, Market Development Director; and Mary Sutton, Associate Marketing Director, for your enthusiastic support and hard work.

To my project editor, Margaret Cleveland, a friend whom I've never met in person, thank you. It's been wonderful working with you. And Brian Orr, I thank you for all the wonderful artwork that you've drawn for all three levels of *All Clear.* And as always, to my daughter Melissa, thank-you for your gut reactions, your natural feel for language, and for always being there.

Dear Student

Welcome to **All Clear! Intro** — Speaking, Listening, Expressions, and Pronunciation in Context. I hope that you have a good time using this book.

As a high-beginning student of English, you know that you need to learn a lot of new vocabulary. In this book, you will learn a lot of vocabulary but you won't learn just words—you will learn groups of words called *expressions.*

Here are some examples of expressions:

- take a walk
- go to bed
- be afraid of
- pick someone up

You will study what these expressions mean. You will also learn how to pronounce them. And you will learn about using these expressions with the correct grammar. You will have a lot of listening and speaking practice, too.

When you use this book, you will talk a lot and have fun.

I wish you good luck, and I hope that you find this book to be "all clear."

Sincerely,

Helen Kalkstein Fragiadakis

Helen Kalkstein Fragiadakis

To the Teacher

All Clear Intro! — Speaking, Listening, Expressions, and Pronunciation in Context is a high-beginning ESL or EFL text that:

- teaches students to recognize and produce high-frequency phrases and expressions

- provides numerous contexts containing natural language

- contextualizes the study of pronunciation by integrating it with the study of expressions

- exposes students to conversational situations that can serve as a basis for conversation practice, often with a cross-cultural focus

- provides many structured and communicative activities for speaking, listening, writing and pronunciation practice.

Question:

What makes this text high-beginning? How is it different from *All Clear Intermediate* and *All Clear Advanced?*

Answer:

The intermediate and advanced texts focus on much more idiomatic language. At the high-beginning level, students need to learn "chunks" of language—common phrases and expressions—that are not as abstract as idioms.

Question:

How were the expressions in this book chosen?

Answer:

For years, as I heard people use common expressions, I wrote them down on scraps of paper wherever I was. The master list lived on my refrigerator door, but I had notes in the living room, by the bed, in my purse, at work, in the car, etc.

My list grew as I spent more and more time teaching the beginning and high-beginning levels. I realized that students needed to learn vocabulary in phrases, not just as individual words. Some expressions in this text are extremely basic, and many high beginners will already have passive knowledge of them. I've included these expressions to help students get the confidence to use them actively too, since they will be armed with the associated information about grammar, pronunciation, and usage.

● *All Clear! Intro* is divided into 8 lessons, 15 appendices and 4 review sections containing a crossword puzzle.

The lessons integrate listening, speaking, pronunciation, grammar, and writing, while focusing on teaching expressions. Throughout each lesson, students are given opportunities to be very active learners and to take responsibility for their own learning. In the middle and at the end of each lesson, they have opportunities to conduct self-assessments. Two additional self-assessment formats appear in Appendices H and I.

Varied activities and numerous visuals are designed to reach students with a range of learning styles. Exercises move from structured to communicative. Role plays, games, dictations, surveys, contact assignments, a jigsaw, and information gap activities are provided. Students are up and out of their seats for Walk & Talk activities.

● It is possible to move through the text in random order. Each lesson is independent, except in one area: pronunciation. If you plan to make pronunciation a substantial component of your course, you might prefer to follow the lessons in order because the pronunciation points build upon one another.

- You might want to start with Lesson 1, as it has more detailed instructions than the other lessons. These instructions are intended to help students understand how to deal with the different parts of the lesson.

- Most activities, from the Warm-Up to the last exercise, can be done in pairs or groups. When students work in groups, you might want to assign roles: leader, reporter, time keeper, participant. Group leaders should make sure that students know each other's names, that everyone participates in a balanced way, and that the group stays on task and completes the activity at hand.

Appendices

The appendices have numerous uses. Some appendices provide supplementary material, such as typical classroom language, a Hot Seat exercise that can be done at any time (especially when you have five to ten minutes of class left), vowel and consonant information, and information about holidays. Some appendices require critical-thinking strategies and become student-created inventories. Other appendices include tapescripts and answer keys.

Cassette Tape

The supplementary cassette tape uses natural speech to present the following from each lesson:

- Opening Dialogue

- Listening Challenges

- Exercise 1—Mini-Dialogues

- Exercise 2—Scene Two

- Exercise 3—Dictation

- Exercise 4—Pronunciation (certain sections)

I hope you and your students enjoy using this text, and I welcome your comments and suggestions.

Helen Kalkstein Fragiadakis
Contra Costa College
San Pablo, California

Icebreaker

Directions

1. At the first class meeting, the students, and maybe also the teacher, fill out the questionnaire below (most likely an adapted form).
2. At the second class meeting, the students "Walk & Talk," using the form on the next page. The items they ask about are taken from the questionnaires that they filled out at the first class meeting.

STUDENT QUESTIONNAIRE

What is your name?   (last)_____   (first) _____

What name do you want everyone to call you in class? _____

Where are you from?   _____

What is your native language? _____

How long have you been in the U.S./Canada? _____

or

Have you ever been in a country where English is the main language?
_____Yes   _____No

If yes, where? _____

What language or languages do you speak at home? _____

Do you work? _____

If yes, what do you do? _____

What classes are you taking now? _____

What do you like to do in your free time?

What is something interesting about you or someone in your family?

What do you want to learn in this class?

Is there anything that you want to tell me about yourself or our class? If yes, please tell me here:

WALK & TALK

Get out of your seat and get to know your classmates. Find out the information in the Walk & Talk activity by talking to at least five different students.

Steps:

● On the lines below, first write the questions you will ask your classmates.

● Check with your teacher to make sure that your questions are correct.

● Get up and ask a student the first question.

—If the student says "no," then say "thank you" and go to another student.

—If the student says "yes," then ask "What is your (first) name?" If necessary, also ask "How do you spell that?" Then write the student's first name on the line at the right, next to the question. Say "thank you" and then ask a different student the next question.

● Continue until you have a name next to each question.

● After everyone has finished, they can sit down again. The teacher will ask who said "yes" to each question and ask them for more information.

Sample questions:

Questions	First Names of students who said *yes*

1. Who is from Mexico?

   Question: Are you from Mexico _____ ? _____

   How do you spell that?

2. Who wants to speak, speak, and speak in this class?

   Question: Do you _____ ? _____

3. Who speaks a little bit of English at home?

   Question: Do you _____ ? _____

4. Who is a cook/manicurist/doctor/ businessperson?

   Question: Are you _____ ? _____

5. Who plays the guitar?

   Question: Do you _____ ? _____

6. Who has four sisters and five brothers?

   Question: Do you _____ ? _____

7. Who speaks Japanese?

   Question: Do you _____ ? _____

Lesson 1 What's Wrong?

Starting a New Class

Warm-Up

In two minutes, write words that show how you feel on the first day or during the first week of class.

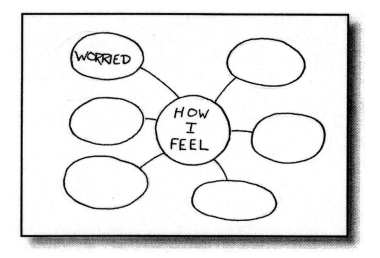

When you finish, put your words in this chart. Under the **+**, put the words that show you feel good. Under the **–**, put the other words. Students can put their words in a chart on the board.

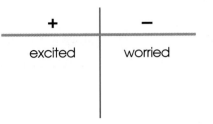

+	**–**
excited	worried

Focused Listening

BEFORE YOU LISTEN

- Look at the cartoon on page 1. It is the first day of school. With a partner, answer, this question: What do you think the two students, Andy and Eric, are talking about?

- Read these five sentences. *Don't give the answers now.* These sentences can be true or false (not true). Or, it may not be possible to know if a sentence is true or false.

  _____ **1.** Eric is worried and shy, and Andy is helping him.

  _____ **2.** Andy is not nervous.

  _____ **3.** Eric will make many friends in this class.

  _____ **4.** The teacher wants students to talk in this class.

  _____ **5.** Eric and Andy are best friends.

AS YOU LISTEN

Think about the five sentences above and the information that you need to get. The dialogue is on the next page, but don't read it now. Just listen.

AFTER YOU LISTEN

T	F	?

- Now complete the "Before You Listen" exercise. On the lines to the left, write **T** for sentences that are true, **F** for sentences that are false, and **?** when it is not possible to know the answer. Check your answers with a partner.

- Listen to the tape again. This time, listen while you read the dialogue on the next page.

- Say the dialogue in pairs.

- Have two volunteers perform the dialogue in front of the class.

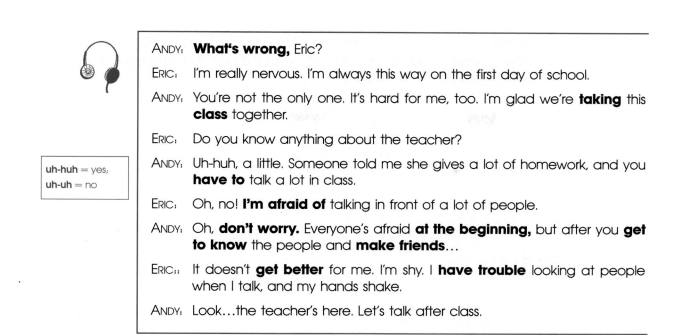

ANDY: **What's wrong,** Eric?

ERIC: I'm really nervous. I'm always this way on the first day of school.

ANDY: You're not the only one. It's hard for me, too. I'm glad we're **taking** this **class** together.

ERIC: Do you know anything about the teacher?

ANDY: Uh-huh, a little. Someone told me she gives a lot of homework, and you **have to** talk a lot in class.

ERIC: Oh, no! **I'm afraid of** talking in front of a lot of people.

ANDY: Oh, **don't worry.** Everyone's afraid **at the beginning,** but after you **get to know** the people and **make friends**...

ERIC: It doesn't **get better** for me. I'm shy. I **have trouble** looking at people when I talk, and my hands shake.

ANDY: Look...the teacher's here. Let's talk after class.

■ Understanding the New Expressions

> *Note:* S1 & S2 = Speaker 1 and Speaker 2

Learn with Others and/or On Your Own

WITH OTHERS

Work with a partner or in a small group.
1. Read the short dialogues and examples from each section aloud.
2. If there is something you don't understand, ask another student for help, or ask your teacher.
3. After you read about each expression and do the *Your Turn* exercise, put an X in the *Yes* or *No* box in the margin to show if you understand. If you put an X in the *No* box, highlight or underline what you don't understand.
4. When your class comes back together as a large group, ask questions about what you don't understand.

ON YOUR OWN

Work on this section carefully. For each expression, put an X in the *Yes* or *No* box to show if you understand the information. If you put an X in the *No* box, then highlight or underline what is still not clear to you. At the next class, your teacher and/or your classmates will answer your questions.

or

List your questions on 3″ x 5″ cards. Give your cards to your teacher at the next class. Your teacher and/or your classmates will answer your questions and give you more examples.

1. Whát's wróng?

> **Note:** You ask this question when you see a person with a problem.
> *Pronunciation Note:* *What* + *is* can become a contraction pronounced as one word: *what's.*

S1: **What's wrong?**
S2: I have a headache.
   I feel sick.
   My test was hard.
   I'm tired.
   My car doesn't work.

Similar Expression: **Whát's wróng with _____?**

S1: **What's wrong with** you? You look tired.
S2: I am tired. I didn't sleep last night.

> **Your Turn:** Think about your friends and family. When do you say, "What's wrong?"
>
> I ask "What's wrong?" when: someone is _____.
>   someone is _____.

2. táke _____ cláss/táke clásses   (past = took)

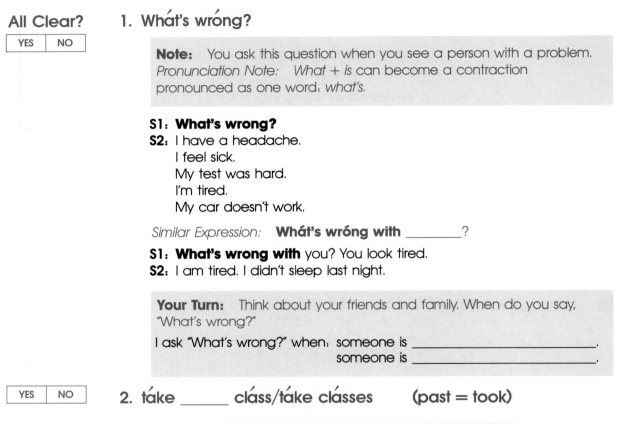

- I**'m taking this class** because it's very interesting.
- I **took that class** last semester.

- **I'm taking:**
    - one **class** because I have a job.
    - three **classes** so I have a lot of homework.

> **Your Turn:** (Answer in full sentences.)
>
> - How many classes are you taking right now?
>
>   I _____.
>
> - What class(es) are you taking?
>
>   I _____.
>
> - Did you take any classes last year?
>
>   (yes)   (no) _____.

YES	NO

3. háve to   (past = had to)

> **Note:**   You say "have to" when you need to do something that is necessary.
>
> **Pronunciation Note:**   You *don't have to* say this, but many native speakers use this pronunciation:
>
>   I/you/we/they "have to" = "hafta"
>   she/he/it "has to" = "hasta"
>
> **Grammar Note:**   After the word *to*, always use the simple form of the verb. For example, it is correct to say, "In school, a student has to go to classes." It is not correct to say, "has to goes," and it is not correct to say "had to went." Look at the two lists below:

In school, you
$\begin{pmatrix} \text{have to} \\ \text{had to} \end{pmatrix}$:
go to classes
study
do homework
talk in class
take tests

a student $\begin{pmatrix} \text{has to} \\ \text{had to} \end{pmatrix}$:
go to classes
study
do homework
talk in class
take tests

> **Your Turn:**   What are three things that teachers have to do?
>
> Teachers have to _____.   A teacher has to _____.
>
>   _____.   _____.
>
>   _____.   _____.

4. be afráid of (+ noun)   (past = was or were)

Pronunciation Note: **Contractions with BE**		
Affirmative	Negative (Present)	Negative (Past)
I am/I'm	I'm not	I wasn't
you are/you're	you're not/you aren't	you weren't
he is/he's	he's not/he isn't	he wasn't
she is/she's	she's not/she isn't	she wasn't
it is/it's	it's not/it isn't	it wasn't
we are/we're	we're not/we aren't	we weren't
they are/they're	they're not/they aren't	they weren't

Be afraid of (+ noun)

- I **'m afraid of**   earthquakes.

- He **isn't afraid of**   you.

- We **are afraid of**   tests.

- She **wasn't afraid of**   the big dog, but she is afraid of it now.

- They **were afraid of**   snakes when they were young.

Be afraid of (+ verbING)

- I **'m not afraid of**   flyING.

- He **is afraid of**   walkING alone at night.

- We **aren't afraid of**   takING the test.

- She **was afraid of**   gettING married, but she isn't afraid now.

- They **weren't afraid of**   talking to the teacher, but they are afraid now.

Your Turn

(1) What are you afraid of? Give examples of things that you are afraid of.

	Nouns	VerbING
I am afraid of	_____	_____
	_____	_____
	_____	_____

(2) What is your partner afraid of?

She/He is afraid of	_____	_____
	_____	_____
	_____	_____

5. Dón't wórry (about)

Pronunciation Note: *Do + not* can become a contraction pronounced as one word: *don't.*

S1: I don't want to fly.
S2: Don't worry! Flying is safe.

S1: You're too young to drive a car.
S2: Don't worry! I know how to drive.

Similar Expression: **be wórried about**

S1: Don't worry about the test. You'll do a good job.
S2: I hope so.

S1: Don't worry about me. I know what to do.
S2: Good. I'm glad to hear that.

S1: I'm worried about my family. There's bad weather in my country right now.
S2: Can you call them?

S1: What's wrong with him?
S2: He**'s worried about** his classes. They are very hard.

Your Turn: Finish these dialogues:

S1: _____.
S2: Don't worry!

S1: What are you worried about?
S2: I'm _____.

6. at the begínning (of)

● I was at a party last Saturday. **At the beginning,** everyone was quiet. But after an hour, the party was noisy.

● **At the beginning of** the party, everyone was quiet.

Opposite = **at the énd (of)**

● The party was quiet at the beginning, but it was noisy **at the end.**

● **At the end of** the party, everyone was happy.

Your Turn

● How do you feel at the beginning of summer?

_____

● How do you feel at the end of summer?

_____

● How do you feel at the beginning of class?

_____

● How do you feel at the end of class?

_____

7. gét to knów (people)   (past = got)

Note: *Get to know* means "start to know more and more about a person."

Teacher: I want to **get to know** you, so I'm going to ask you a few questions, OK?
Student: OK.
Teacher: Where are you from? What do you do? Do you like living here?

S1: How's your class?

S2: It's great. I'm getting to know more students, so I'm happy.

Your Turn: Listening Challenge

Listen to the short conversation on the tape. Two people are asking questions because they want to get to know each other. Which question is first? Which question is second? As you hear each question, put a number on the line at the left.

__1__ Where are you from?	____ And you?
____ Why not?	____ How about you?
____ What's your name?	____ When did you come to the US?
____ Do you like it here?	

YES	NO

8. máke friénds (with)   (past = made)

Note: First you meet a person, and then maybe you will make friends with him or her. To do this, you ask questions to get to know each other, and if you like each other, you "make friends."

S1: I'm not happy here. I don't know anyone.

S2: You need to **make friends.** When you have some friends, you'll feel better.

S1: It's hard to **make friends with** people here. People say they will call or visit, but they don't.

S2: I know. But you can **make friends.** You just need time.

Your Turn

● Does it take a long time for you to make friends, or do you make friends easily (with no trouble)?

_____

● When you were younger, did you make friends with people that your parents liked or didn't like?

_____

YES	NO

9. gét bétter = improve   (past = got)

S1: It is very hard for me to speak English.

S2: Don't worry. Your English will **get better** every day.

S1: I wasn't happy here when I first arrived, but my life **got better** and I'm happy now.

S2: That's good to hear.

● I had a bad cold, but I **got better** quickly.

Your Turn: What are some ways that your life can get better?

My life can get better if: _____

_____

_____

10. háve tróuble (___ING) = have problems (___ING)
    (past = had)

I **have trouble**   talkING in class.
                         speakING English.

She **has problems**   sleepING when it is noisy.
                         understandING people when they speak fast.

Your Turn: What do you have trouble doing?

I have trouble   _____.

_____.

_____.

Note: You can also say "have trouble with (something)" and "have trouble when ___:"

● I often have trouble *with* my homework.

● She has trouble *when* she speaks English.

Any Questions?

Take out a piece of paper. Do not write your name on it. On one side of the paper, write what you think is the most interesting information that you have learned in this lesson. On the other side of the paper, write any questions you have about what you studied or talked about in class. Your teacher will collect this paper and then answer your questions the next time you meet.

For Example

● The most interesting thing I learned is that a lot of people are nervous in class. I'm nervous, too. I also learned to say "make friends." Before, I said "meet friends."

● What is the difference between "get to know" and "make friends"?

Exercises

1. Mini-Dialogues

Match the lines in A with the lines in B. You will then make mini-dialogues (very short conversations).

To check this exercise, say each mini-dialogue with a partner. One student will read a line from A, and another student will answer with a line from B.

A

____1. I'm afraid of talking on the phone in English.
____2. It's hard to get to know people when you live in a big city.
____3. What's wrong?
____4. Why are you taking this class?
____5. At the beginning, I always said, "Sorry, I don't speak English."
____6. I don't want to leave! I made a lot of friends here.

B

a. Because I want my English to get better.
b. I have trouble getting to know people, too.
c. We all have to write to each other.
d. Don't be afraid. You can do it.
e. I'm afraid of dogs. Can you take him away?
f. But now what do you say?

2. Scene Two — Listening

Now it's after class, and Andy and Eric are having lunch in the cafeteria. They are talking about their first class.

As you listen to the tape, fill in the blanks with the expressions that you hear. Be sure to use a capital letter at the beginning of a sentence. When you finish, perform the dialogue with a partner.

ERIC: (1) _____, Andy?

ANDY: Now (2) _____ the class. The teacher said we (3) _____ do a lot of homework.

ERIC: (4) _____! I can help you. I think the class will be good, and we are going to (5) _____ there.

ANDY: Eric, you're funny. (6) _____, you (7) _____ _____, and now you're fine. What happened?

ERIC: I don't know. I enjoyed talking to the students, and I want to (8) _____ them. Maybe I won't (9) _____ talking in this class. I wasn't very nervous after the first five minutes.

ANDY: That's great. I can see you're happy that you (10) _____ this class. I think your English will (11) _____ very quickly.

ERIC: I hope you're right.

3. Dictation

Your teacher or one of your classmates will read the dictation for this lesson from Appendix C, or you will listen to the dictation on the tape. You will hear the dictation three times. First, just listen. Second, as you listen, write the dictation on a separate sheet of paper. Third, as you listen, check what you have written.

period .
comma ,
apostrophe '
open quote "
closed quote "

After you listen,
Proofread

● Did you indent the first line of each paragraph?
● Does every sentence start with a capital letter?
● Do the names have capital letters?
● Does each sentence end with a period?

Check yourself

After you check your dictation, look at your mistakes. What do you have to be more careful about next time?

____spelling   ____vocabulary

____plurals   ____verb tenses

____subject-verb agreement   ____punctuation

Other: _____

4. Pronunciation—Part 1: Stress

These are the expressions from this lesson:

WHAT'S WRONG	at the BEGINNING
TAKING THIS CLASS	GET to KNOW
HAVE to	MAKE FRIENDS
be AFRAID of	GET BETTER
DON'T WORRY	HAVE TROUBLE

Notice the words that are not in capital letters. These words are usually not strong, or stressed (emphasized):

to	(from the infinitive, for example: have "to talk")
be	(verb "be" and am/is/are/was/were)
of, at	(prepositions)
the	(article)

Now practice saying the first part of the introductory dialogue. Make the capitalized words stronger than the other words.

ANDY: WHAT'S WRONG, Eric?

ERIC: I'm REALLY NERVOUS. I'm ALWAYS THIS WAY on the FIRST DAY of SCHOOL.

ANDY: You're not the ONLY one. It's HARD for me, TOO. I'm GLAD we're TAKING this CLASS TOGETHER.

ERIC: Do you KNOW ANYTHING about the TEACHER?

ANDY: UH-HUH, a LITTLE. SOMEONE TOLD me she GIVES a LOT of HOMEWORK, and you HAVE to TALK a LOT in CLASS.

PRONUNCIATION & LISTENING PRACTICE

Listen to the tape and

● say each expression. Make the words *to, be, of , at* and *the* less strong (weaker) than the other words.

● practice repeating each sentence of the dialogue.

Pronunciation—Part 2: "Hafta" & "Hasta"

Have to is often pronounced "hafta" and *has to* is often pronounced "hasta."

It is important for you to understand this pronunciation when you listen to English, but you do not have to pronounce *have to* in these ways.

Listen to the dialogue again and notice how *have to* is pronounced.

5. Walk & Talk

Use the following dialogue to get to know at least four of your classmates. Walk around the room and complete the dialogue with different students.

A: Hi, I'm ____. What's your name?
B: I'm ____. It's nice to meet you.
A: Nice to meet you, too. Where are you from?
B: I'm from ____. How about you?
A: I come from ____. Do you have trouble speaking English?
B: Sometimes. That's why I'm taking this class.
A: It's the same for me. Well, it was nice talking to you. See you later.
B: See you.

6. Write

Write sentences about the four students you talked to in Exercise 5.
For example:

1. Mario is from...
2. Mari comes from...
3. Nai sometimes has trouble...
4. Katia is taking this class because...

_____

_____

_____

_____

_____

_____

_____

_____

Notes are...
(1) short—not full sentences.
(2) just a few words so you can remember information later.

7. Group Survey

1. Get into groups of three or four. Choose one student to be the leader. This person will ask the questions.

Put the first names of the group members on the top lines.

The leader will interview one person at a time. Each student in the group will write short notes in the spaces under each person's name.

	Student Name	Student Name	Student Name	Student Name
Questions	/_____/	/_____/	/_____/	/_____/
1. Why are you taking this class?				
2. Is there anything about this class that you are afraid of? If yes, what?				
3. What do you have to do so your listening & speaking will get better?				
4. What do you have the most trouble with in English?				

2. Choose one person to be the Reporter. This person can tell the class some of the answers to the questions. It is not necessary to say students' names when giving this report.

Examples:
Students in my group are taking this class because . . .
One person in my group is afraid of . . .
Two people in my group are going to . . . so their listening and speaking will get better.
We have trouble with . . .

8. Tic-Tac-Toe — Play & Write

Directions

a. Your teacher will put the tic-tac-toe lines on the board, with expressions in the nine spaces.

b. The class should be divided into two teams, *X* and *O*. Flip a coin (choose "heads or tails") to see which team goes first.

c. To get an *X* or an *O* in a space, a team has to make a sentence with the expression in that space. The sentence should be correct in grammar and meaning. Team members can plan what they will say for up to 30 seconds. Students should take turns giving the answers.

d. The first team to get three *X*'s or *O*'s in a straight line wins. The line can be horizontal, vertical, or diagonal.

e. When you finish a game, if there are any expressions that are not covered by *X*'s or *O*'s, you can keep them for another game. You can add other expressions to the spaces already used and play again.

at the beginning of	taking this class	get to know
have to	make friends with	be afraid of
get better	have trouble	at the end of

After you play tic-tac-toe, write sentences using all of the expressions. When you write, start every sentence with a capital letter, think about spelling, and be careful with verb tenses and other grammar that you are studying.

9. Expression Clusters & Charts

1. Look at the words in Appendix D on pages 165 and 166. Find expressions from this lesson that have these words, and write the expressions on the lines. For example, on the first line under the word *take* in Appendix D, write the expression *take a class.*

   A cluster is a group, and you are making clusters of expressions that have the same words. This will help you remember what you are studying.

   You will do this when you finish each lesson. And you should add other expressions that are not in this book. When you finish your course, you will have a lot of expression clusters.

2. Look at Appendix E on page 167. Use this chart to write down expressions from this lesson that you hear or read outside of class.

3. Look at Appendix F on page 169. Use this chart to write down new expressions from outside of class. These are not expressions from this book. You may find them on TV, on the radio, in the movies, on T-shirts, on bumper stickers, and in advertisements.

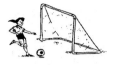

10. Goal Post

Can you now use the new expressions when you listen and speak? Put *(a)* or *(b)* next to each expression in the chart below:

	For Listening (a) I know what this expression means. (b) I'm not sure what this expression means.	**For Speaking** (a) I am comfortable saying this when I speak. (b) I am not comfortable saying this when I speak.
what's wrong	_____	_____
take ___ class	_____	_____
have to	_____	_____
be afraid of	_____	_____
don't worry	_____	_____
worry about	_____	_____
at the beginning	_____	_____
at the end	_____	_____
get to know	_____	_____
make friends	_____	_____
get better	_____	_____
have trouble	_____	_____

If you gave any expression a *(b)*, be sure to ask your teacher or a classmate for help.

Before you start the next lesson, answer these questions about this lesson:

● What did you do to learn new expressions?

● What activities helped you the most?

Lesson **2** *Who's This?*

Making Telephone Invitations

Warm-Up

Circle what you think are the correct answers:

1. When you want to ask who is calling you, you can say:
   (a) Who are you?   (b) Who's this?
2. When you say your name on the phone, you can say:
   (a) I am ____.   (b) This is ____.
3. When you ask someone on the phone to wait, you can say:
   (a) Wait, please.   (b) Just a minute.

Focused Listening

BEFORE YOU LISTEN

- Look at the cartoon above. Alex is calling someone. With a partner, answer these questions: Who is Alex calling? Why is he calling her?

- Read the nine questions below, *but don't answer them now.*

1. Is Alex calling Sara? _____

2. Is Anna Sara's sister? _____

3. Does Alex want to go to the movies with Sara? _____

4. Does Alex want to go to the movies with Anna? _____

5. Can Sara go to the movies on Friday night? _____

6. Can she go to the movies on Saturday night? _____

7. Is Alex going to drive? _____

8. Is Sara going to drive? _____

9. Are Sara and Anna going to have dinner soon? _____

AS YOU LISTEN

Think about the information that you need to get. The dialogue is below, but don't read it now. Just listen.

AFTER YOU LISTEN

- Answer the nine questions under Before You Listen. Use short yes-or-no answers with *is, does, can,* or *are.* For example, write *Yes, he is* for number 1. Check your answers with a partner.

- Listen to the tape again, but this time, listen while you read the dialogue.

- Say the dialogue in groups of three.

- Have three volunteers perform the dialogue in front of the class.

SARA'S SISTER, ANNA: Hello.

ALEX: Hi, Sara.

ANNA: **Who's this?**

ALEX: **It's** Alex.

ANNA: Oh, hi, Alex. **This is** Anna. **Hold on** a minute and I'll get Sara. . . Sara, **it's for you!** . . .

SARA: **I'll be right there**. . . . Alex? Hi!

ALEX: Hi, Sara. Want to go to the movies Friday night?

SARA: I'm really sorry, but I **can't make it** Friday night. . . How about Saturday?

ALEX: Sure. **Why don't** I **pick you up** at 7:00?

SARA: **That sounds** great. Oh, Alex, I'm sorry. My parents are calling me for dinner and I have to **get off.** See you Saturday.

ALEX: Great. See you. Bye.

■ Understanding the New Expressions

Learn with Others and/or On Your Own

WITH OTHERS

Work with a partner or in a small group.

ON YOUR OWN

Work on this section carefully, and then for each expression put an X in the *Yes* or *No* box in the margin to show if you understand the information.

(For more detailed directions, see page 3.)

All Clear?

YES	NO

1. Whó's thís? = Who is this?

> **Note:** You can ask this when you don't know who is calling on the phone. When you don't know who is *at the door*, you ask, "Who's there?" or "Who is it?"

S1: Hi. Can (or May) I please speak to Daniel? (or: Can/May I speak to Daniel, please?)
S2: Who's this?
S1: It's Melissa.

Similar Expressions: **Whó's cálling? Can I ásk whó's cálling? May I ásk whó's cálling?**

These expressions are formal. They are usually used by businesses and people who don't know each other.

All Clear?

Your Turn: What are the best questions to ask in these telephone conversations?

A: Computers Incorporated.

B: Hello. May I please speak to Ms. Williams?

A: _____?

B: This is her son.

A: One moment, please.

A: Hello.

B: Hi. Can I speak to Steve, please?

A: _____?

B: It's his sister.

A: Sure. Just a sec. (Just a second.)

YES	NO

2. It's ___´ ; This is ___´ .

Note: You say "It's___" or "This is ___" after someone asks you, "Who's this?" It is not correct to say "I am" when you give your name on the phone.

S1: Hello.

S2: Hello. May I speak to Alex Nicholas, please?

S1: **This is** Alex. (Or: This is he. Or: Speaking.)

S2: This is Bill from Computer Incorporated. I'm calling to tell you that your computer is ready.

S1: Hello.

S2: Hello. Is Sara there? (Or: May I please speak to Sara?)

S1: Who's this?

S2: **It's** (or This is) Alex.

S1: Just a moment.

Your Turn

Have a phone conversation with a partner. Use the dialogue above as a model. Your partner will answer the phone, and you will ask to speak to a famous person. Your partner will ask who you are.

A: Hello.

B: _____

A: _____

B: _____

A: _____

3. hold ón   (past = held)

Note: Say this when a person calls you and you want that person to wait a minute.

S1: Hello.
S2: Hello. This is Sara. May I speak to Daniel, please?
S1: Sure. **Hold on** and I'll get him.

Sometimes when you are on the phone with a business, you will hear this:

● Doctor's Office. Can you hold?

● Please hold, and someone will be with you shortly (soon).

Related Telephone Expressions:

● **ánswer the phóne** or ánswer it (When you pronounce "answer," remember the "w" is not pronounced.)

● **gét the phóne** or gét it = answer the phone or answer it

● **hang úp** = finish your call and put the receiver (the part that you hold next to your ear) back on the phone   (past = hung)

- Daniel, the phone's ringing. Can you **answer (get) it?**

- Alex, when are you going to **hang up?** I need to use the phone!

Note: You can also "hang up" clothes in a closet on a clothes hanger.

Your Turn: Finish these three dialogues with "hold on," "answer the phone," and "hang up."

A: Wait! Don't _____! I want to talk to him.
B: OK. Don't worry. He wants to talk to you, too.

A: Anna. Can you _____? My hands are wet.
B: Sure. Hello. . .

A: Hi, can I please speak to Jon?
B: Sure. _____.

YES	NO

4. It's for (yóu)! = The phone call is for you.

S1: Hurry up! **It's for you!** It think it's long distance.
S2: I'm coming.

S1: Who is it? **Is it** for me?
S2: No, **it's for me.**

Similar Expressions to announce that a phone call is for someone:

- _____(person's name)! There's a call for you!

- _____(person's name)! Phone's for you!

- _____(person's name)! Telephone!

Your Turn

Get into groups of three and write a phone conversation. Use your real names. The phone rings. The first student says "Hello." The second student asks for the third student. The first student says "Just a minute" and calls the third student.

(Ring)

1st student _____: Hello.
(name)

2nd student_____, _____?
(name)

1st student _____: Just a minute.
(name)

_____, _____!
(name of third student)

| YES | NO |

5. I'll be right thére. = I'm cóming.

Note: You cannot change this sentence. It is not correct to say, "I'll be right there in five minutes." When you say, "I'll be right there," you are saying that you will be there immediately.

S1: Hurry! The phone's for you.
S2: **I'll be right there.**

Your Turn: Say these lines with a partner.

A	B
1. It's time to go.	I'll be right there.
2. We're leaving.	I'll be right there.
3. Everyone is ready for dinner.	I'll be right there.
4. Can you help me with my homework?	I'll be right there.
5. _____.	I'll be right there.

Who's This?

6. can/can't make it = can/can't go somewhere

S1: I **can make it** on Monday, but not on Tuesday.
S2: Monday's fine.

S1: There's a great concert on Saturday night.
S2: On Saturday night? Oh I'm sorry. I **can't make it.** I already have plans.
S1: That's too bad.

> **Your Turn:** Complete this conversation with a partner. Follow the example above.
>
> A: There's a _____.
>
> B: On _____? Oh, I'm sorry. _____.
> _____.
> (give a reason)
>
> A: That's too bad. Maybe next time.

7. Why don't ____?

> **Note:** This is a way to give ideas about things to do.

S1: **Why don't we** go swimming, and then take a walk?
S2: Great idea!

S1: **Why don't you** go to the bank, and I'll go to the post office?
S2: I don't know. Let's go together.

> **Your Turn: Listening Challenge**
>
> Listen to the tape. You will hear six sentences. After you hear each sentence, give a suggestion from the list. Write the letter of the suggestion next to the number of the sentence that you hear.
>
> **Suggestions**
>
> _c_ 1.   a. Why don't you go to bed?
>
> ____ 2.   b. Why don't you get something to eat?
>
> ____ 3.   c. Why don't we go to the beach?
>
> ____ 4.   d. Why don't you take lessons?
>
> ____ 5.   e. Why don't they go to the movies?
>
> ____ 6.   f. Why don't we study together?

8. pick (someone) úp = get someone, often by car

S1: I'll **pick you up** in front of the library at 4 o'clock, OK?

S2: Thanks a lot. That will be a big help.

● She **picked up** her brother.

● She **picked her brother up** at school.

● She **picked him up.**

Don't say, "She picked up him." Pronouns have to go in the middle.

pick	me	up
	you	
	him	
	her	
	it	
	them	
	us	

Your Turn

Put a √ next to the correct sentences. Put an X next to the incorrect sentences, and then correct these sentences.

Corrections

_√_ 1. I'll pick you up later.

_X_ 2. I'll pick up you tomorrow.   I'll pick you up tomorrow.

____ 3. She pick her children up
every day after school.   _____

____ 4. She picks them up every
day after school.   _____

____ 5. My friend pick him up yesterday.   _____

____ 6. Can you pick up me at 5?   _____

Who's This?

9. Thát sóunds ___!

Note: This is what you can say when something you hear about sounds good or bad.

S1: I can pick you up at 10, and then we can go to the beach.
S2: That sounds great!

S1: I was in traffic for three hours.
S2: That sounds terrible!

S1: The movie was about life in a college dorm.
S2: That sounds interesting.

Your Turn: Respond with "That sounds great/terrible/interesting."

That sounds . . .

● It rained for two weeks when I was on vacation. _____

● After lunch, we went to the park and then we went to a movie. _____

● I met a lot of people from many different countries. _____

● _____. _____

10. get óff (the phone) = hang úp (see number 3) (past = got)

● When are you going to **get off?** I need the phone!

● I'm sorry, but I have to **get off** the phone. It's already midnight.

Note: You can also **get off** a bike, a horse, a bus, a train, and an airplane, but you "get out of" a car.

Your Turn
Is there anyone in your family who often doesn't want to get off the phone? If yes, who? What do you say to him or her when you want to use the phone?

Any Questions?

Take out a piece of paper. Do not write your name on it. On one side of the paper, write what you think is the most interesting information that you have learned in this lesson. On the other side of the paper, write any questions you have about what you studied or talked about in class. Your teacher will collect this paper and then answer your questions the next time you meet.

Exercises

1. Mini-Dialogues

Match the lines in A with the lines in B. You will then make mini-dialogues.

To check this exercise, say each mini-dialogue with a partner. One student will read a line from A, and another student will answer with a line from B.

A	**B**
____1. Can you come on Sunday?	a. I'll be right there.
____2. Bill. It's for you!	b. OK. I'll talk to you tomorrow. Bye.
____3. Why don't I pick you up after school?	c. Who's this?
	d. Sure. I'll get it.
____4. Sorry. I have to get off.	e. I'm sorry, but I can't make it.
____5. Hello. Can I please speak to Ann?	f. Thank you. That's really nice of you.
____6. Can you answer the phone?	

2. Scene Two — Listening

The following is a telephone conversation between Alex and Sara. They are talking on Sunday, the day after they had dinner together.

As you listen to the tape, fill in the blanks with the expressions that you hear. Be sure to use a capital letter at the beginning of a sentence. When you finish, perform the dialogue with a partner.

SARA'S SISTER:	Hello.
ALEX:	Hi. Can I speak to Sara, please?
SARA'S SISTER:	(1) _____?
ALEX:	(2) _____ Alex.
SARA:	(3) _____ a second. . . Sara!
	(4) _____! It's Alex.

SARA:	(5) _____ . . . Hi, Alex.
ALEX:	Hi, Sara. How are you doing?
SARA:	Fine. How about you?
ALEX:	Pretty good. I had a really great time last night.
SARA:	I did too. That's a great restaurant.
ALEX:	I know. (6) _____ we go back there next weekend?
SARA:	(7) _____ great. When?
ALEX:	Is Friday OK? I can (8) _____ at 7:00 again.
SARA:	Why don't *I* drive this time? I'll pick *you* up at 7:00.
ALEX:	That's fine with me. I'll be waiting for you. Take care. . .
SARA:	Alex? Wait. . . Don't (9) _____ . There's one more thing. Last week, *you* paid for dinner. This time, *I* want to pay.
ALEX:	Sara! No!
SARA:	Yes! Listen, . . .

3. Dictation

Your teacher or one of your classmates will read the dictation for this lesson from Appendix C, or you will listen to the dictation on the tape. You will hear the dictation three times. First, just listen. Second, as you listen, write the dictation on a separate sheet of paper. Third, as you listen, check what you have written.

period .
comma ,
apostrophe '
open quote "
closed quote "
question mark ?
exclamation
  point !

After you listen,
Proofread

● Did you indent the first line of each paragraph?
● Does every sentence start with a capital letter?
● Do all the names and days have capital letters?
● Does each sentence end with a period, question mark, or exclamation point?

Check yourself

After you check your dictation, look at your mistakes. What do you have to be more careful about next time?

___spelling   ___vocabulary

___plurals   ___verb tenses

___subject-verb agreement   ___punctuation

Other: _____

4. Pronunciation—Part 1: Stress in Two-Word Verbs

In this lesson, you learned four "two-word verbs": *hold on, hang up, pick up,* and *get off.* Two-word verbs are verbs with two (or three) words. Usually, the second part of the verb gets the most stress.

When you say these words, stress (emphasize) the second word:

> hold ON/held ON; hang UP/hung UP;
> pick UP/picked UP; get OFF/got OFF

PRONUNCIATION & LISTENING PRACTICE

Say these sentences:

* Hold ON a minute, and I'll get Sara.
* Alex, when are you going to hang UP?
* Why don't I pick you UP at 7?
* My parents are calling me for dinner, and I have to get OFF.

Do the following:

* Look at the dialogue at the beginning of this lesson and also look at the dialogue in Exercise 2. Put stress marks over the second word when you see these expressions: *hold on, hang up, pick up* and *get off.*
* Listen to the tape of the two dialogues. Listen to how the expressions are said. Are the second parts of these two-word verbs stronger? Repeat the lines of these dialogues after the speakers.

Pronunciation—Part 2: Contractions

Contractions are two words put together to form one word. Native speakers of English use many contractions when they speak, and that may be why you sometimes don't understand what you hear.

Here are examples from this lesson. Practice saying both the full forms and the contractions.

Full Forms	Contractions
1. who is	who's
2. it is	it's
3. I will	I'll
4. cannot	can't
5. do not	don't

Now say:

1. Who's this?
2. It's Alex.
3. It's for you.
4. I'll be right there.
5. I can't make it on Saturday.
6. Why don't I pick you up?

With a partner, practice the dialogues on pages X and Y. Stress the second parts of two-word verbs and use the contractions that you practiced above.

5. Walk & Talk

Walk around the room and ask your classmates the following question. As they talk, take short notes below.

Question: In Exercise 2, Sara told Alex that she wanted to drive and that she wanted to pay for dinner. Is it OK for a woman to drive and pay for a man? Why or why not?

Names of students who said "yes"	Reasons	Names of students who said "no"	Reasons

6. Write

Write sentences about what students said to you in Exercise 5. Use these forms:

___thinks it is good for a woman to drive a man because ___.

___thinks it is good for a woman to pay for a man because ___.

___thinks it is not good for a woman to drive a man because ___.

___thinks it is not good for a woman to pay for a man because ___.

1.

2.

3.

4.

5.

7. Role Play

Get into groups of four. Two people will watch and listen, and the other two people will be "phone partners." The phone partners will put their chairs back-to-back, just as you see in the cartoon.

The phone partners will role-play a phone call. Partner A will call partner B and invite him or her to go somewhere this weekend. Partner B can't make it on Saturday, but can make it on Sunday. As they talk, the partners should look at the list of expressions in Exercise 10 and try to use them.

After the phone partners finish this role play, the other two students can talk about what happened and about how the partners used the new expressions. Then, the other two students will become the new phone partners.

Starting lines
R i n g . . .
S1: Hello.
S2: Hi. Can I please speak to . . . ?
S1: . . .

8. Tic-Tac-Toe — Play & Write

In tic-tac-toe, to get an *X* or an *O* in a space, you need to make a sentence that is correct in grammar and meaning. Here is a game with expressions from Lesson 2. (See page X for more detailed directions.)

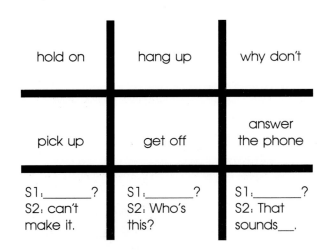

hold on	hang up	why don't
pick up	get off	answer the phone
S1:_____? S2: can't make it.	S1:_____? S2: Who's this?	S1:_____? S2: That sounds__.

After you play tic-tac-toe, write sentences using all of the expressions. When you write, start every sentence with a capital letter, think about spelling, and be careful with verb tenses and other grammar that you are studying.

9. Expression Clusters & Charts

1. Look at the words in Appendix D on pages 165 to 166. Find expressions from this lesson that have these words, and write the expressions on the lines. For example, on the first line under the word *get* in Appendix D, write the expression *get the phone*.
2. Look at Appendix E on page 167. Use this chart to write down expressions from this or other lessons that you hear or read outside of class.
3. Look at Appendix F on page 169. Use this chart to write down new expressions from outside of class. These are not expressions from this book. You may find them on TV, on the radio, in the movies, on T-shirts, on bumper stickers, and in advertisements.

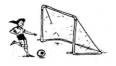

10. Goal Post

Can you now use the new expressions when you listen and speak? Put *(a)* or *(b)* next to each expression in the chart below:

	For Listening (a) I know what this expression means. (b) I'm not sure what this expression means.	**For Speaking** (a) I am comfortable saying this when I speak. (b) I am not comfortable saying this when I speak.
What's this?	_____	_____
Who's calling?	_____	_____
it's. . ., this is. . .	_____	_____
hold on	_____	_____
answer the phone	_____	_____
hang up	_____	_____
It's for you!	_____	_____
I'll be right there.	_____	_____
can't make it	_____	_____
why don't. . .	_____	_____
pick up	_____	_____
that sounds____	_____	_____
get off	_____	_____

If you gave any expression a *(b)*, be sure to ask your teacher or a classmate for help.

Before you start the next lesson, answer these questions about this lesson:

● What did you do to learn new expressions?

● What activities helped you the most?

Crossword Puzzle for Lessons 1 and 2

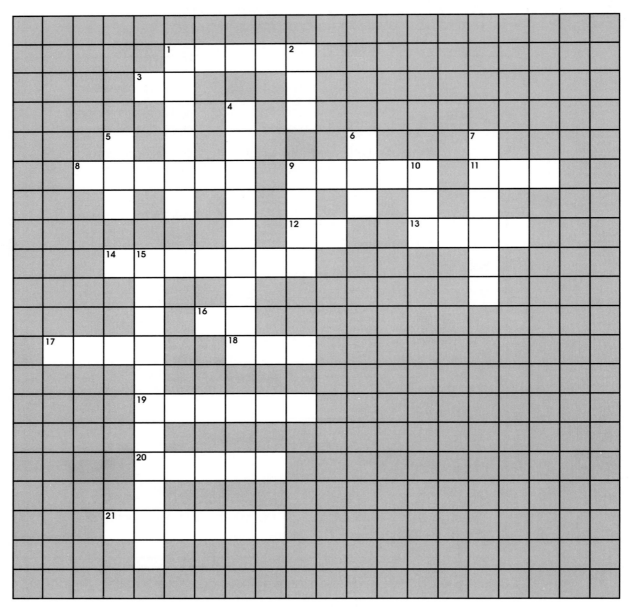

Across

1. Don't worry ___ this class.
3. I'm not afraid ___dogs.
8. She's ___three classes.
9. I'll be right ___.
11. Sorry, I need to get ___ the phone and do my homework.
12. This ___ Janet.

Down

1. Everyone is ___ of earthquakes.
2. At ___ end of the movie, everyone was crying.
4. At the ___, English was very hard.
5. We ___ to drive five hours yesterday.
6. When are you going to ___ off the phone? I need it!

Across

13. Why ___ I pick you up in front of the theater?
14. She made a lot of ___ in her class.
16. Can you hold ___ a minute?
17. We can't ___ it tomorrow. We're sorry.
18. Last year we ___ to know many people at our school.
19. I'm sorry you're sick. I hope you get ___ soon.
20. I'll be ___ there.
21. Can you ___ the phone?

Down

7. That ___ wonderful.
9. Who's ___ ?
10. I'm almost at the ___ of the book.
15. I have trouble ___ these expressions.

Lesson 3 Let's Go Away for the Weekend

Making Plans for the Weekend

Warm-Up

What do you like to do when you have free time? Look at the 12 activities below. Next to each, write a number (1, 2, 3, 4, or 5) to show if you don't like it, if it's just ok, or if you like it a lot.

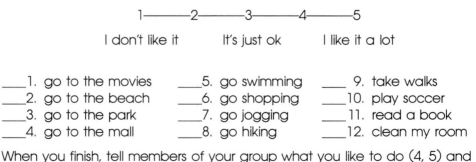

1————2————3————4————5

I don't like it   It's just ok   I like it a lot

___1. go to the movies   ___5. go swimming   ___ 9. take walks
___2. go to the beach   ___6. go shopping   ___10. play soccer
___3. go to the park   ___7. go jogging   ___11. read a book
___4. go to the mall   ___8. go hiking   ___12. clean my room

When you finish, tell members of your group what you like to do (4, 5) and what you don't like to do (1, 2). For example, you can say:

When I have free time,   I like to _____.

I don't like to _____.

Focused Listening

Look at the cartoon on page 39 and read these five sentences.

I agree	I disagree

BEFORE YOU LISTEN

Look at the cartoon on page 39 and read these five sentences. *Don't write the answers now.*

_____ 1. Peter wants to go to the beach.

_____ 2. Alice is surprised because Peter wants to go to the beach in the winter.

_____ 3. Alice doesn't want to go away for the weekend.

_____ 4. There will be many people at the beach.

_____ 5. Peter and Alice will go away for three days.

AS YOU LISTEN

Listen to the dialogue to see if you agree or disagree with these sentences.

AFTER YOU LISTEN

- Write *I agree* next to a sentence if it is right. Write *I disagree* next to a sentence if it is wrong. (Be careful. Don't write *I am agree.*) Check your answers with a partner.

- Listen to the tape again, but this time, listen while you read the dialogue below.

- Say the dialogue in pairs.

- Have two volunteers perform the dialogue in front of the class.

PETER: You know, we have a three-day weekend next month. Do you want to **go away?**

ALICE: That's a great idea! Where do you want to go?

PETER: To the beach.

ALICE: The beach in the winter?

PETER: We don't have to **go swimming.** We can **take walks** on the beach.

ALICE: But **what else** can we do?

PETER: Oh, there are **plenty of** things to do. We can read, go to the movies. I need to relax, don't you?

ALICE: I sure do. You're right. The beach is a good idea. And it won't **be crowded.** Do you think we need to **make a reservation** anywhere?

PETER: No, I don't think so. There are **lots of** places to stay.

■ Understanding the New Expressions

Learn with Others and/or On Your Own

WITH OTHERS

Work with a partner or in a small group.

ON YOUR OWN

Work on this section carefully, and then for each expression put an X in the *Yes* or *No* box in the margin to show if you understand the information.

(For more detailed directions, see page 3.)

All Clear?

YES	NO

1. gó awá y (for)   (past = went)

Note: When you go away, you leave home and sleep in a different place for one or more nights.

Pronunciation Note: When you say *went away*, connect the two words so they sound like one word: went away.

S1:   What's the suitcase for?
S2:   I**'m going away** for a few days. My sister is getting married.
S1:   Have a great trip!

S1:   Ruth, we**'re going away** for the weekend. Can you take care of the dog?
S2:   Sure. No problem.

S1:   How was your weekend?
S2:   It was great. We **went away** for a few days.

All Clear?

Similar Expressions: **gó on a tríp** (to), **táke a tríp** (to), gó (to)

S1: What are you going to do this weekend?
S2: We're going to **go on a trip** to
take a trip to } Disneyland.
go to

S1: Where did they go?
S2: They
went on a trip to
took a trip to } Disneyland.
went to

> **Your Turn:** With a partner, answer these questions:
> 1. Do you like to go away? Why or why not?
> 2. When you go away, do you usually
>   (a) stay with friends and relatives?
>   (b) stay at a hotel or motel?
>   (c) go camping?
>   Why?

YES	NO

2. gó swímming

S1: It's such a hot day! Do you want to **go swimming** after class?
S2: That's a good idea. Do you want to go to the beach or to a pool?

> **Note:** Use "go _____ing" to talk about activities that you do, not places. It is not correct to say "go *to* _____ing."

Activity	Place
go shopping	go to a store; go to a mall
go jogging	go to a park
go fishing	go to a river
go swimming	go to a swimming pool or a beach
go hiking	go to the mountains
go ice skating	go to a skating rink
go dancing	go to a club

Your Turn: Fill in the blanks with *go* or *go to*:

1. _____ the mountains   5. _____ shopping

2. _____ a club   6. _____ dancing

3. _____ ice skating   7. _____ swimming

4. _____ a river   8. _____ a store

YES	NO

3. táke wálks   (past = took)

Note: You take walks for pleasure or exercise. You can *take a walk* to the park, but you don't *take a walk* to work. You *walk* to work.

S1:   What do you do to get exercise?
S2:   Well, I go swimming when I can, and I **take** (long) **walks**.

Singular: **táke a wálk = gó for a wálk**

● It's a beautiful evening. Do you want to **take a walk** around the block?

● We **took** a long **walk** yesterday afternoon. It was great.

Your Turn
Write two sentences with these expressions. Remember to use *took* if you are talking about the past.

(1) take walks

_____

(2) take a walk

_____

YES	NO

4. whát élse = what more/what other things

S1:   Let's see...we have bread, salad, and juice. **What else** do we need?
S2:   Uh, I think we need some rice, but that's all.

All Clear?

S1: What did you do over the weekend?
S2: Well, let's see. I cleaned my house and did my laundry.
S1: **What else** did you do?
S2: Oh, yes! I almost forgot. I went to a great party.
S1: I'm glad you did something that was fun.

> **Your Turn**
>
> Here is the beginning of a dialogue. Complete the dialogue using the simple present tense because you are talking about what you do in *every* class.
>
> **S1:** What do you do in your class?
> **S2:** Oh, we listen to a tape and we talk a lot.
> **S1:** _____ do you do?
> **S2:** We _____ and _____.

YES	NO

5. plénty of = more than enough (more than you need)

S1: I think we need to buy more rice.
S2: No, we don't. Look — we have **plenty of** rice right here.
S1: Really? Oh, I didn't see it.

S1: Mom, I'm bored. I have nothing to do.
S2: Oh, there are **plenty of** things to do. You can clean your room, take out the garbage, and walk the dog. When you finish doing all that, tell me, and I'm sure I'll find more for you to do.

YES	NO

6. be crówded = be full of people

● This restaurant **is crowded.** Let's go somewhere else.

● In the winter, the beach **isn't crowded.**

● Let's go home. This party **is** too **crowded.**

● I'm tired. I had to stand on the bus all the way home because it **was** so **crowded.**

  Contrast the noun: a crowd; crowds

● There is a big **crowd** near that car. Maybe someone famous is in the car.

● I don't like **crowds,** so I want to stay home on New Year's Eve.

Your Turn

What kinds of places can be crowded? _____

_____

_____

How do you feel when you are in a crowd? I feel _____ in a crowd.

(adjective)

All Clear?
| YES | NO |

7. máke a reservátion (for)　　(past = made)

S1: Hello. Rivoli's.

S2: Hi. I'd like to **make a reservation** for Saturday night.

S1: Sure. What time?

S2: 7:30 for six people.

S1: And your name?

S2: Rose.

S1: OK. That will be six people for 7:30 on Saturday night. See you then.

S2: Thanks a lot.

Your Turn: Use the dialogue above as an example to make a reservation at a restaurant.

S1: Hello. _____.

S2: Hi. I'd like to make a reservation for _____.

S1: Sure. _____?

S2: _____.

S1: And your name?

S2: _____.

S1: OK. That will be

_____. See you then.

S2: Thanks a lot.

Your Turn: Listening Challenge

Listen to the telephone conversation on the tape. Someone is making a reservation at a restaurant. After you listen, answer these questions.

1. Why is the caller making a reservation? _____
2. Who will go to the restaurant with the caller? _____
3. Where does the caller want to sit in the restaurant? _____
4. When is the reservation for? _____

| YES | NO |

8. lóts of = a lót of = many/much

Pronunciation Note: *Lots of* is often pronounced "lotsa" or "lotsuv."

S1: We had **lots of** (a lot of) homework last night, didn't we?

S2: Uh-huh. I worked on it for two hours!

S1: How was your weekend?

S2: Oh, we had **lots of** (a lot of) fun. We went hiking and swimming. It was great. Do you want to come with us the next time we go?

Your Turn

What do you like?

_____1. lots of friends

_____2. lots of tests

_____3. lots of books to read

_____4. lots of traffic (cars on the road)

_____5. lots of free time

Any Questions?

Take out a piece of paper. Do not write your name on it. On one side of the paper, write what you think is the most interesting information that you have learned in this lesson. On the other side of the paper, write any questions you have about what you studied or talked about in class. Your teacher will collect this paper and then answer your questions the next time you meet.

Exercises

1. Mini-Dialogues

Match the lines in A with the lines in B. You will then make mini-dialogues.

To check this exercise, say each mini-dialogue with a partner. One student will read a line from A, and another student will answer with a line from B.

A	**B**
____1. We went shopping and then we went out to lunch.	a. That's a good idea. I'll call there now.
____2. Do we need to leave now?	b. No, we have plenty of time. We can leave in a half hour.
____3. That restaurant is always crowded. Do you think we need to make a reservation?	c. It's not crowded everywhere. I'm sure we can find a quiet place to go.
____4. I'm full. Does anyone want to take a walk with me?	d. What else did you do?
____5. Lots of people want to go away in the summer. That's why it's so crowded everywhere.	e. Great idea. I'll be right there.

2. Scene Two — Listening

The following is a conversation between Peter and his friend Bonnie. Peter is telling Bonnie about the great weekend he had with his wife, Alice.

As you listen to the tape, fill in the blanks with the expressions that you hear. When you finish, perform the dialogue with a partner.

PETER: Hi, Bonnie. How was your weekend?

BONNIE: Pretty good. I stayed home and relaxed. How about you? Did you and Alice (1) _____?

PETER: Uh-huh. We found a small town near the beach and stayed in a nice motel for three nights. It was great.

BONNIE: What did you do at the beach? Wasn't it cold?

PETER: Yeah, a little. We didn't (2) _____.
But we (3) _____. And we got (4) _____ fresh air.

BONNIE: At this time of year, it probably (5) _____
_____.

PETER: No, it wasn't.

BONNIE: So, (6) _____ did you do?

PETER: Let's see. . . on Saturday night, we (7) _____
_____ at a club, and on Sunday we
(8) _____. It was a lot of fun.

BONNIE: It sounds like you had a great weekend. Can you give me the name of the town? Maybe Eddie and I will go there sometime.

3. Dictation

Your teacher or one of your classmates will read the dictation for this lesson from Appendix C, or you will listen to the dictation on the tape. You will hear the dictation three times. First, just listen. Second, as you listen, write the dictation on a separate sheet of paper. Third, as you listen, check what you have written.

period .
comma ,

Proofread
● Did you indent the first line of the paragraph?
● Does every sentence start with a capital letter?
● Do the names have capital letters?
● Does each sentence end with a period?

Check yourself

After you check your dictation, look at your mistakes. What do you have to be more careful about next time?

___spelling   ___vocabulary

___plurals   ___verb tenses

___subject-verb agreement   ___punctuation

Other: _____

4. Pronunciation — Sentence Stress

In Lesson 1, you learned that some words (for example, prepositions and articles) in English are not stressed (not said strongly).

Other words need to be said strongly. These words (such as nouns and adjectives) have a lot of information and need to be strong and clear. To understand which words need to be stressed or not stressed, look at the boxes on the next page. All of the words come from the dialogue on page 40.

USUALLY STRESS*

Nouns	Main Verbs	Negative Helping Verbs	Adjectives
weekend	know	don't	three-day
month	have	won't	next
idea	want		great
beach	go		right
winter	take		good
swimming	do		crowded
walks	read		
plenty	need		
things	relax		
movies	think		
reservation	make		
lots	stay		
places			

*Also stress:
- Question words (who, what, where, when, why, how)
- Demonstrative pronouns (this, that, these, those)
- Pronouns and forms of be when they are the last word in a sentence
- Adverbs

USUALLY DON"T STRESS

Forms of be	Prepositions	Articles	Helping Verbs	Pronouns	Conjunctions
is	to	a(n)	do	you	but
are	in	the	can	we	and
be	on			I	(or)
	of			it	(so)

PRONUNCIATION & LISTENING PRACTICE

- Say the following lines from the dialogue. The stressed words are in capital letters.

- Listen again to the tape of the dialogue. Repeat after the speakers.

1. You KNOW,
   we HAVE a THREE-DAY WEEKEND
   NEXT MONTH.
   Do you WANT to
   go AWAY?

2. THAT's a GREAT IDEA!
   WHERE do you WANT to GO?

3. To the BEACH.

4. The BEACH in WINTER?

5. We DON'T HAVE to
   GO SWIMMING.
   We can TAKE WALKS on the BEACH.

6. But WHAT ELSE can we DO?

7. Oh, THERE are PLENTY of THINGS
   to DO.
   We can READ,
   GO to the MOVIES.
   I NEED to RELAX,
   DON'T YOU?

8. I SURE DO.
   You're RIGHT.
   The BEACH is a GOOD IDEA.
   And it WON'T be CROWDED.
   Do you THINK
   we NEED to MAKE a RESERVATION ANYWHERE?

9. NO, I DON'T THINK SO.
   THERE are LOTS of PLACES to STAY.

5. Walk & Talk

A. Imagine that it is Friday. First, complete this dialogue. (You can get ideas from this lesson's warm-up exercise.) Then, get up and walk around the room. Say the dialogue with different students. Your dialogues will be different. Take turns being Speaker A or Speaker B.

Don't write—just speak, and be sure to look at the people you talk to. If you don't understand what someone says, say "Could you please repeat that?"

A: What are you going to do this weekend?

B: I'm going to _____.

A: What else are you going to do?

B: I'm going to _____. How about you?

A: I'm going to _____ and _____.

B: That sounds _____ (great/interesting). Have a good time!

A: You too. Nice talking to you. See you.

B: It was nice talking to you, too.

B. Imagine that it is Monday. First, complete this dialogue. Then, get up and walk around the room. Say the dialogue with different students. Your dialogues will be different. Remember to use the past tense.

A: How was your weekend?

B: It was _____. (great, pretty good, OK, terrible)

A: What did you do?

B: I _____.

A: What else did you do?

B: I _____.

A: Did you have a good time?

B: _____. (Yes, it was fun/interesting. OR: No, not really.) How about you? What did you do?

A: I _____.

B: That sounds _____. Well, it was nice talking to you. See you.

A: See you.

6. Write

Write what your classmates said to you in Exercise 5:

First, write sentences about what three students are going to do this weekend. Use the students' names.

-
-
-

Second, write sentences about what three students did last weekend:

-
-
-

7. Info Gap

Imagine that the summer is over and now you are back at school. You see a friend and talk about your summer.

One of you will be Speaker 1 and the other will be Speaker 2. Speaker 1 will look at page 193, and Speaker 2 will look at page 194. You will have different information to give each other.

When you finish, find a new partner and tell that person about your first partner's summer.

8. Tic-Tac-Toe — Play & Write

In tic-tac-toe, to get an *X* or an *O* in a space, you need to make a sentence that is correct in grammar and meaning. Here is a game with expressions from Lesson 3. (See page 15–16 for more detailed directions.)

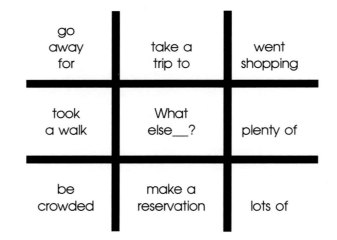

go away for	take a trip to	went shopping
took a walk	What else __?	plenty of
be crowded	make a reservation	lots of

After you play tic-tac-toe, write sentences using all of the expressions. When you write, start every sentence with a capital letter, think about spelling, and be careful with verb tenses and other grammar that you are studying.

9. Expression Clusters & Charts

1. Add expressions from this lesson to the expression clusters in Appendix D.
2. When you hear or read expressions that you have studied in class, add them to Appendix E.
3. Write down new expressions from outside of class in Appendix F.

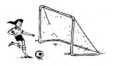

10. Goal Post

Can you now use the new expressions when you listen and speak? Put (a) or (b) next to each expression in the chart below:

	For Listening (a) I know what this expression means. (b) I'm not sure what this expression means.	**For Speaking** (a) I am comfortable saying this when I speak. (b) I am not comfortable saying this when I speak.
go away	_____	_____
go on a trip	_____	_____
take a trip	_____	_____
go ____ ing	_____	_____
take walks	_____	_____
take a walk	_____	_____
What else ___?	_____	_____
plenty of	_____	_____
be crowded	_____	_____
make a reservation	_____	_____
lots of	_____	_____
a lot of	_____	_____

If you gave any expression a (b), be sure to ask your teacher or a classmate for help.

Before you start the next lesson, answer these questions about this lesson:

● What did you do to learn new expressions?

● What activities helped you the most?

Lesson 4 Wake Up!

Describing Your Daily Routine

Warm-Up

In the morning, what do you do first? What do you do second?

Number the following. Put the numbers on the lines at the left. Everyone will have different answers.

__1__ a. wake up

____ b. wash your face

____ c. get up

____ d. brush your teeth

____ e. take a shower

____ f. go to school or go to work

____ g. get dressed (put on clothes)

____ h. eat breakfast

____ i. shave (Of course, not everyone does this.)

Focused Listening

BEFORE YOU LISTEN

Look at the cartoon on page 57. What do you think is the problem?

AS YOU LISTEN

Try to find out why Tom doesn't want to get up.

AFTER YOU LISTEN

● Give three reasons why Tom doesn't want to get up.

He doesn't want to get up because _____.

_____.

_____.

● Listen to the tape again, but this time, listen while you read the dialogue.

● Say the dialogue in pairs.

● Have two volunteers perform the dialogue in front of the class.

ROOMMATE 1:	**Wake up,** Tom! Don't you have to go to the airport?
ROOMMATE 2:	Yeah, I'll **get up** in five minutes. I don't want to **get out of bed** — it's so early.
ROOMMATE 1:	Well, I**'m going back to sleep.** I hope you won't miss your plane. **Have a good trip.**
ROOMMATE 2:	Thanks. Oh, why did I **go to bed** so late last night? It's so hard to **get up,** and it's so cold and dark. But I need to get up now and **take a shower.** What time is it. . . ? 6 o'clock? Oh, no! I'm late. I **don't have time for** a shower. I have to **get dressed** and get to the airport right away.

■ **Understanding the New Expressions**

Learn with Others and/or On Your Own

WITH OTHERS

Work with a partner or in a small group.

ON YOUR OWN

Work on this section carefully, and then for each expression put an X in the *Yes* or *No* box in the margin to show if you understand the information.

(For more detailed directions, see page 3.)

1. wake úp = open your eyes after sleeping (past = woke up)

> **Pronunciation Note:** Remember to stress the second part of this two-word verb.

S1: What time do you **wake up** every day?
S2: At about 7. How about you?

S1: I like weekends because I can **wake up** late.
S2: What time do you usually **wake up**?
S1: About 11.

S1: I didn't sleep well last night.
S2: Why not?
S1: I **woke up** a lot because my roommate was snoring.

wake someone up = wake another person

wake	me	up
	you	
	him	
	her	
	it	
	us	
	them	

S1:   Shh! The baby's sleeping. Don't **wake her up**!
S2:   Sorry. I didn't know.

S1:   I'm going to take a nap. Can you **wake me up** in an hour?
S2:   Sure.

Opposite: **fáll asléep**   (past = fell)

●   Children often **fall asleep** when they are riding in cars.

●   The movie was very boring, so I **fell asleep**.

●   I went to bed at 11:00, but I **fell asleep** around 1:00 because I was thinking a lot about my life.

Your Turn

Ask your partner these questions about this morning. Write the answers on the right.

Questions	Answers
1. What time did you wake up this morning?	I woke up at _____.
2. Did a person wake you up?	Yes No
3. Did an alarm clock wake you up?	Yes No
4. What time did you fall asleep last night?	I fell asleep at around _____.

| YES | NO |

2. get úp = get out of bed after you wake up (past = got up)

S1: **Get up,** Sandy! You'll be late for school!
S2: I am up, Mom.

S1: I'm going to bed early tonight because I have to **get up** early tomorrow.
S2: Why?
S1: I have an appointment.

S1: What time did you wake up this morning?
S2: I woke up at 6, but I **got up** at 7.
S1: Why?
S2: I was listening to the radio. It was nice.

S1: You look sleepy.
S2: I am. I **got up** at 5 this morning.
S1: Really? Why?
S2: I started an exercise program.

Opposite: **gó to béd** (see number 6)

Your Turn: Ask your partner these questions. Write the answers on the right.

Questions	Answers
1. What time did you get up this morning?	I got up at _____.
2. What time do you usually get up on weekdays?	I usually get up at _____
3. What time do you usually get up on weekends?	I usually get up at _____

3. get óut of béd

> **Note:** It is not correct to say get out of *the* bed.

S1: Every night their three-year-old son **gets out of bed** and goes into his parents' bed.

S2: Is that OK with his parents?

● It's so cold in here! I don't want to **get out of bed**.

Your Turn

Question: When is it hard for you to get out of bed?

Answer: It's hard for me to get out of bed when _____.

_____.

_____.

4. go báck to sléep = go to sleep again after you wake up (past = went)

S1: Dad, wake up! I had a bad dream.

S2: It was a dream. Now, **go back to sleep.** Everything is OK.

S1: Why are you watching TV at 3 in the morning?

S2: I woke up and I can't **go back to sleep.**

S1: Do you want some tea?

S2: That sounds nice. Thanks.

Your Turn

When you wake up in the middle of the night, is it usually hard for you to go back to sleep? If it is hard, what can you do to get sleepy?

5. Háve a góod (great) tríp!

> **Note:** You say this when someone is going to leave and travel somewhere.

S1: Bye! See you in a month.

S2: See you. **Have a good trip!**

S1: Do you have your ticket?

S2: Yes.

S1:	Do you have enough money?
S2:	Uh-huh.
S1:	Do you have your toothbrush?
S2:	Listen, I have to go now.
S1:	Bye. **Have a good trip!** Call me when you get there.

Similar Expression: **táke a tríp** (See Lesson 3) (past = took)

S1:	What are you going to do this weekend?
S2:	We're going to **take a trip** to the mountains.

Your Turn

Question: Imagine that someone just gave you $1,000. You want to use the money to take a trip. Where do you want to go?

Answer: I want to go to _____.

I want to take a trip to _____.

YES	NO

6. gó to béd   (past = went)

Note: It is not correct to say go to *the* bed.

S1:	I'm tired. I'm **going to bed.**
S2:	But it's only 9 o'clock!
S1:	I know, but last night I **went to bed** very late.

● When I take a nap in the afternoon, I can't **go to bed** early.

All Clear?

YES	NO

7. néed to

S1: I **need to** go to the airport.
S2: What time? I can take you.
S1: Really? Thanks!

Grammar Note: Put the simple form of the verb after *to.*

● We **need to**   sleep.

be healthy.

learn English.

If you don't use *to,* then you should put a noun after the word *need.*

● We need   money.

clean air.

time to learn English.

8. táke a shówer   (past = took)

Similar Expression: **take a bath**

S1:   What do you do after you get up?
S2:   I wash my face, brush my teeth, and **take a shower.** Sometimes I take a bath.

Your Turn

Ask your partner these questions:

(1) What do you like better—to take a shower or to take a bath?

(2) How long are you usually in a shower? in a bath?

(3) Do you sing in the shower?

9. háve tíme for (something) háve tíme to (do something)

S1:   Do you **have time** for a cup of coffee?
S2:   Sure. Great idea!

S1:   Sorry, I **don't have time** to eat breakfast. I'm late.
S2:   Here, take some toast with you.
S1:   Thanks. See you.

All Clear?   Look at when you use "have time FOR" and "have time TO."

Have time FOR something	Have time TO DO something
Do you have time for a cup of coffee?	Do you have time to drink a cup of coffee?
I don't have time for breakfast.	I don't have time to eat breakfast.

Your Turn

Are you a very busy person? On the left, write three things that you don't have time for, and on the right, write three things that you don't have time to do.

I don't have time for (noun)	I don't have time to (verb)
_____	_____
_____	_____
_____	_____

YES	NO

10. gét dréssed = put on your clothes

S1:   Let's go!
S2:   Wait! I have to **get dressed** first. I'm still in my pajamas.

Similar Expression: **put ón** (specific clothes)   (past = put)

- He is only three years old, and he is learning to **get dressed.**

- He is only three years old, and
  he is learning to **put on**

  his clothes

  his socks

  his shoes

  his pants

  his shirt

  his jacket.

Note: When you say "get dressed," you mean that a person puts on all of his or her clothes. When you say "put on," you mean that a person puts on specific clothes, such as socks:

> She is getting dressed. (general)
>
> She is putting on her socks. (specific clothes)

Note: When you "get dressed" or "put something on," you are using an action with your hands to put clothes on your body. After you "get dressed" or "put something on," you are wearing something. When you "wear" clothes, they are already on you. There is no action.

Opposite: gét undréssed = take óff (your clothes)

- He is only three years old, and he is learning to **get undressed.**

- He is only three years old, and
  he is learning to **take off**

  his clothes

  his socks

  his shoes

  his pants

  his shirt

  his jacket.

Note about "put on" and "take off": When you use an object pronoun (me, you, him, her, it, us, them) with these two-word verbs, put the pronoun in the middle. See the box below:

Yes	Yes	Yes	No
put on your shoes	put your shoes on	put them on	put on them
put on your shirt	put your shirt on	put it on	put on it
take off your shoes	take your shoes off	take them off	take off them
take off your shirt	take your shirt off	take it off	take off it

Your Turn

(a) Next to each sentence, write C if the sentence is correct, and I if the sentence is incorrect.

_c_ 1. He put on his shoes.

____ 2. He put on his jacket.

____ 3. He put his jacket on.

____ 4. He put it on.

____ 5. He put on it.

____ 6. The child took off his shirt.

____ 7. The child took it off.

____ 8. The child took off it.

____ 9. The child took his shirt off.

____ 10. The child got dressed.

(b) **Your Turn: Listening Challenge**

This is a dictation. Write the sentences that you hear. Every sentence ends with an exclamation point (!).

1. _____

2. _____

3. _____

4. _____

5. _____

Any Questions?

Take out a piece of paper. Do not write your name on it. On one side of the paper, write what you think is the most interesting information that you have learned in this lesson. On the other side of the paper, write any questions you have about what you studied or talked about in class. Your teacher will collect this paper and then answer your questions the next time you meet.

Exercises

1. Mini-Dialogues

Match the lines in A with the lines in B. You will then make mini-dialogues.

To check this exercise, say each mini-dialogue with a partner. One student will read a line from A, and another student will answer with a line from B.

A	**B**
____1. Wake up! You're late!	a. Isn't that sweet. She fell asleep.
____2. What time did you go to bed last night?	b. Why don't you put on a sweater?
____3. Sorry, I don't have time to talk. I have to go to the airport.	c. Can you wait five minutes? I need to get dressed.
____4. It's time to go.	d. It's too cold to get up.
____5. It's really cold in here.	e. Have a great trip!
____6. It's really hot in here.	f. Why don't you take off your sweater?
____7. Look at the baby.	g. Very late.

2. Scene Two

Tom is now back from his trip. He is talking to his roommate.

As you listen to the tape, fill in the blanks with the expressions that you hear. When you finish, perform the dialogue with a partner.

ROOMMATE 1:	So, how was your trip?
ROOMMATE 2:	Great. My cousin's wedding was really nice, and I saw a lot of my friends and relatives.
ROOMMATE 1:	Did you miss your plane?
ROOMMATE 2:	You know, I almost did. I was really late because I didn't want to (1) _____. Remember?
ROOMMATE 1:	Yeah. It was really cold and dark in here.
ROOMMATE 2:	But I (2) _____ on the plane, and then I felt better. When I got to my parent's house, it was great. We (3) _____ to talk and relax. I (4) _____ some of my old clothes and worked in the garden. Then I (5) _____ and (6) _____ for the wedding.
ROOMMATE 1:	What did you wear? Do you have any nice clothes?
ROOMMATE 2:	Sure, I do. I have a suit, you know.
ROOMMATE 1:	I don't believe it. You (7) _____ show me some pictures of you in a suit. I know you only in blue jeans.
ROOMMATE 2:	I'll have some pictures next week. You'll see.

period .
comma ,

3. Dictation

Your teacher or one of your classmates will read the dictation for this lesson from Appendix C, or you will listen to the dictation on the tape. You will hear the dictation three times. First, just listen. Second, as you listen, write the dictation on a separate sheet of paper. Third, as you listen, check what you have written.

Proofread

● Did you indent the first line of each paragraph?
● Does every sentence start with a capital letter?
● Does the name have a capital letter?
● Do the sentences end with a period?

Check yourself

After you check your dictation, look at your mistakes. What do you have to be more careful about next time?

___spelling   ___vocabulary

___plurals   ___verb tenses

___subject-verb agreement   ___punctuation

Other: _____

4. Pronunciation – Intonation

In Lessons 1, 2, and 3, you learned that it is important to stress some words in English. This helps people understand what a speaker thinks is important.

Intonation also helps people understand what a speaker thinks is important.

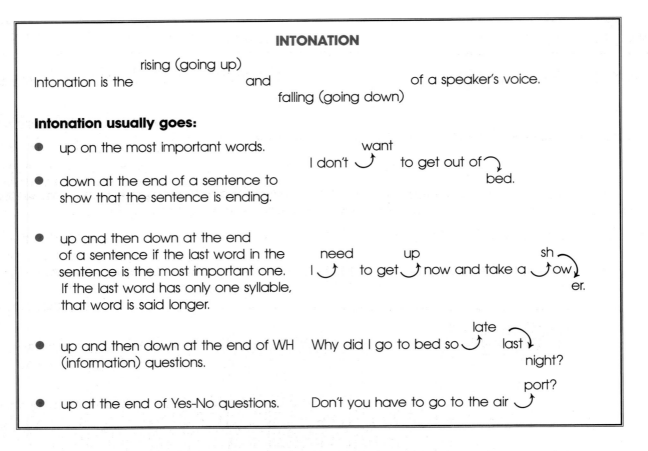

INTONATION

Intonation is the rising (going up) and falling (going down) of a speaker's voice.

Intonation usually goes:

- up on the most important words.

  I don't *want* to get out of bed.

- down at the end of a sentence to show that the sentence is ending.

- up and then down at the end of a sentence if the last word in the sentence is the most important one. If the last word has only one syllable, that word is said longer.

  I *need* to get *up* now and take a *shower.*

- up and then down at the end of WH (information) questions.

  Why did I go to bed so *late* *last* night?

- up at the end of Yes-No questions.

  Don't you have to go to the air *port?*

Step 1: Read the dialogue silently and imagine your voice going up and down. Move your hand up and down to show rising and falling intonation.

Step 2: Say the dialogue with a partner, paying special attention to the rising and falling of your voice.

Step 3: Listen to the tape. Do you hear the speakers' voices going up and down?

Step 4: Say the dialogue with a partner again.

ROOMMATE 1: Wake *up,* Tom! Don't you have to go to the air *port?*

ROOMMATE 2: Yeah, I'll get *up* in five *min utes.* I don't *want* to get out of bed—it's so *early.*

ROOMMATE 1: Well, I'm going back to *sleep.* I *hope* you won't *miss* your *plane.*

Lesson 4

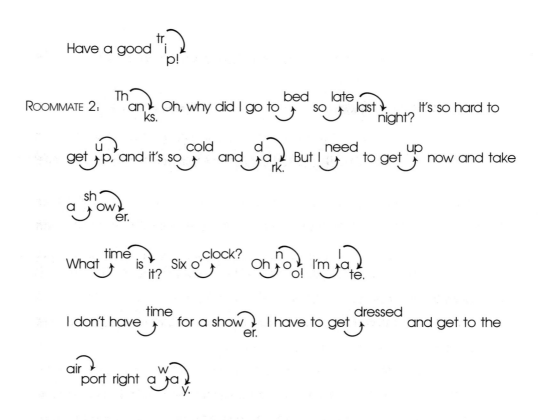

Have a good tri p!

ROOMMATE 2: Thanks. Oh, why did I go to bed so late last night? It's so hard to get up, and it's so cold and dark. But I need to get up now and take a shower.

What time is it? Six o'clock? Oh no! I'm late.

I don't have time for a shower. I have to get dressed and get to the airport right away.

5. Walk & Talk — Sleep Survey

Ask three to five of your classmates these questions. Take very short notes in the spaces. Write the students' names on the right. After you collect the information, do Exercise 6.

Grammar Note
- Use simple present tense because you are talking about a habit, something that you repeat (every day, every weekend). For example, I usually get up at 7:30 on weekdays.

- Use the preposition *at* when you give a time (at 7 o'clock) and use the preposition *on* when you give a day (ON weekdays, ON Sundays).

Names

1. What time do you usually get up on weekdays?

-
-
-
-
-

2. What time do you usually get up on weekends? _____

-
-
-
-
-

3. What time do you usually go to bed on weekdays?
-
-
-
-
-

4. What time do you usually go to bed on weekends?
-
-
-
-
-

5. How many hours of sleep do you need every night?
-
-
-
-
-

6. How many hours of sleep do you usually get every night?
-
-
-
-
-

7. Do you often feel tired?
-
-

-
-
-

8. If you said "yes" to question 7, then what can you do to feel better?
-
-
-
-
-

6. Write

Complete these sentences about the students you talked to in Exercise 5. Give times or numbers in 1, 3, 5, 7, 9, 10, and 11. Give students' names in numbers 2, 4, 6, and 8.

1. Most of the students get up between ____ and ____ on weekdays.

2. _____ gets up the earliest, and _____ gets up the latest on weekdays.

3. Most of the students get up between ____ and ____ on weekends.

4. _____ gets up the latest on weekends.

5. Most of the students go to bed between ____ and ____ on weeknights.

6. _____ goes to bed the earliest, and _____ goes to bed the latest on weeknights.

7. Most of the students go to bed between ____ and ____ on weekends.

8. _____ goes to bed the latest on weekends.

9. Most of the students need between ____ and ____ hours of sleep every night.

10. Most of the students get about ____ hours of sleep every night.

11. ____ out of five students often feel tired.

12. Students can feel better if they

   _____ .

   (To answer this question, see Exercise 5, number 8.)

- Compare your sentences to the sentences that other students in your class wrote.

- Answer this question: Do most students in your class usually get enough sleep?

7. Contact Assignment

With a partner, ask three native speakers of English these questions. You can ask people in your school, at a library or store, or in your neighborhood. You do not need to walk up to strangers on the street.

Introduce yourself like this. You can practice saying this in class:

Hi. We're from _____ and ___ and we're studying English. We have a homework assignment to ask eight short questions about what time people usually get up and go to bed. Do you have a minute to answer our questions?

Be sure to look directly at the people you are talking to. You can take short notes, but don't just look at your book. Also, don't let the people read the questions. You need to ask the questions so that you can practice speaking English with native speakers.

1. What time do you usually get up on weekdays?
   -
   -
   -

2. What time do you usually get up on weekends?
   -
   -
   -

3. What time do you usually go to bed on weekdays?
   -
   -
   -

4. What time do you usually go to bed on weekends?
   -
   -
   -

5. How many hours of sleep do you need every night?
   -
   -
   -

6. How many hours of sleep do you usually get every night?
   -
   -
   -

7. Do you often feel tired?

- ●

- ●

- ●

8. If you said "yes" to question 7, then what can you do to feel better?

- ●

- ●

- ●

After you get the information from the three people, answer these questions:

1. Do the people you talked to usually get enough sleep?___Yes ___No

2. If they don't get enough sleep, what did they say they need to do to feel better?

3. When you said you were studying English and you asked people to talk to you, what did they say?

4. Did the native speakers understand your questions?
___always   ___usually   ___sometimes   ___rarely

5. How much did you understand when the native speakers answered your questions? _____%

6. How did you feel when you talked to the three native speakers?

7. If you do this kind of activity again, would you do anything differently? What?

8. Tic-Tac-Toe — Play & Write

In tic-tac-toe, to get an *X* or an *O* in a space, you need to make a sentence that is correct in grammar and meaning. Here is a game with expressions from Lesson 4. (See pages 15–16 for more detailed directions.)

wake up	get up	go back to sleep
go to bed	need to	take a shower
have time for	have time to	get dressed

After you play tic-tac-toe, write sentences using all of the expressions. When you write, start every sentence with a capital letter, think about spelling, and be careful with verb tenses and other grammar that you are studying.

9. Expression Clusters & Charts

1. Add expressions from this lesson to the expression clusters in Appendix D.
2. When you hear or read expressions that you have studied in class, add them to Appendix E.
3. Write down new expressions from outside of class in Appendix F.

10. Goal Post

Can you now use the new expressions when you listen and speak? Put (a) or (b) next to each expression in the chart below:

	For Listening	**For Speaking**
	(a) I know what this expression means.	(a) I am comfortable saying this when I speak.
	(b) I'm not sure what this expression means.	(b) I am not comfortable saying this when I speak.
wake up	_____	_____
fall asleep	_____	_____
get up	_____	_____
get out of bed	_____	_____
go back to sleep	_____	_____
have a good trip	_____	_____
take a trip	_____	_____
go to bed	_____	_____
need to	_____	_____
take a shower	_____	_____
take a bath	_____	_____
have time for	_____	_____
get dressed	_____	_____
get undressed	_____	_____
put on	_____	_____
take off	_____	_____

If you gave any expression a (b), be sure to ask your teacher or a classmate for help.

Before you start the next lesson, answer these questions about this lesson.

● What did you do to learn new expressions?

● What activities helped you the most?

Crossword Puzzle for Lessons 3 and 4

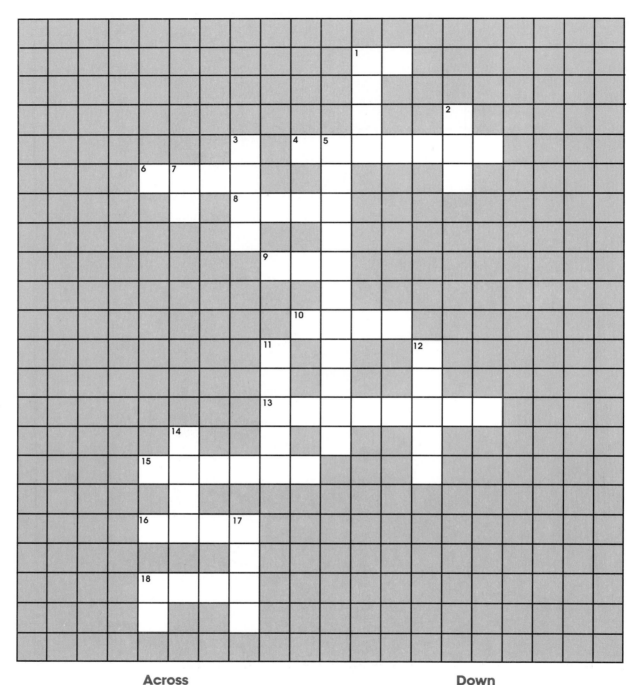

Across

1. We need ____ study a lot.
4. She got ____ really fast because she woke up late.
6. I'm tired. I ____ up at 6.

Down

1. Do you want to ____ a trip with us?
2. It's time to go to ____.
3. The baby ____ asleep on the plane.
5. I'd like to make a ____ for ten for dinner.

Across

8. The party was fun. There were ___ of people there.
9. Do you have time ___ a cup of coffee?
10. See you. I'm going ___ to sleep.
13. Do you want to go ___ on Saturday?
15. Stay for dinner. We have ___ of food.
16. We ___ away for two weeks and had a great time.
18. We ___ a long walk and now we feel a lot better.

Down

7. Sometimes it's hard to get out ___ bed.
11. The beach ___ crowded so we had a good time.
12. We're ___ on a trip for a few days. Can you watch the dog?
14. What ___ do you want to do?
17. Do you want to ___ a trip with us?
18. We need ___ study a lot.

Lesson 5 Are You Ready to Order?

Ordering in a Restaurant

Warm-Up

These are things that people say in a restaurant. Write *W* next to the lines that a waiter or waitress will say, and *C* next to the lines that a customer will say.

_____ 1. I'll be right with you.

_____ 2. Can I get you anything to drink?

_____ 3. We have some specials tonight.

_____ 4. Are you ready to order?

_____ 5. What is the soup of the day?

_____ 6. What kind of salad dressing do you have?

_____ 7. How would you like your hamburger?

_____ 8. Would you like anything else?

_____ 9. Can we have some more water, please?

_____ 10. Can we have the check, please?

Focused Listening

Look at the cartoon on page 83 and then read these five questions. *Don't answer the questions now.*

Question	Short Answer	How Do You Know?
1. Do the brother and sister see each other a lot?		
2. Is this a special day?		
3. Is this the brother's first time in this restaurant?		
4. Who is going to pay for lunch?		
5. Who is shy?		

AS YOU LISTEN

Listen to the dialogue to find the short answers to these questions.

AFTER YOU LISTEN

- Give short answers to the five questions under Before You Listen.
- Listen to the tape again, but this time, listen while you read the dialogue on the next page.
- Say the dialogue in groups of three.
- Have three volunteers perform the dialogue in front of the class.

SISTER:	Oh, this is so nice. What a great birthday present!
BROTHER:	I'm glad you like it. I was thinking, you know, we never really have time to just sit and talk. . .
SISTER:	And now we have two hours! And this is a really nice place.
BROTHER:	Yeah, I come here **once in a while.**
SISTER:	What are you going to have?
BROTHER:	Um. . . I'm not sure yet. But you order **whatever you want.** It's your birthday.
SISTER:	Whatever I want? OK. But please don't sing Happy Birthday when we have dessert. If you do, I'll go under the table.
BROTHER:	You'll never change. Always so shy.
SISTER:	Well, that's me. Anyway, I think **I'll have** the chicken caesar salad. What are you going to have?
BROTHER:	The salad sounds good. But I'm going to have soup too because I**'m** really **hungry.**

❖ ❖ ❖ ❖ ❖

WAITRESS:	Hi, **are you ready to order?**
BROTHER:	Uh-huh. I think so.
SISTER:	I **would like** the chicken caesar salad.
WAITRESS:	Anything to drink?
SISTER:	Just water **for now.**
WAITRESS:	And **how about you?**
BROTHER:	I'll have the same, but I'd also like the vegetable soup.
WAITRESS:	**Will that be all?**
BROTHER:	Uh-huh. **That's all** for now.
WAITRESS:	OK. I'll be right back with your soup.
BROTHER:	Thanks.

Learn with Others and/or On Your Own

WITH OTHERS

Work with a partner or in a small group.

ON YOUR OWN

Work on this section carefully, and then for each expression put an X in the *Yes* or *No* box in the margin to show if you understand the information.

(For more detailed directions, see page 3.)

All Clear?

YES	NO

1. ónce in a whíle = sometimes

Note: *Once in a while* can be an answer to the question, "How often. . . ?"

S1: How often do you come to this restaurant?
S2: Oh, **once in a while.** When I want to celebrate something special.

S1: Do you speak English when you're not in class?
S2: Do I speak English when I'm not in class? Ha! That's a very interesting question. Well, I have to say I speak English just **once in a while** because we don't speak English at home. But I watch TV a lot.

Your Turn: Circle your answers

1. How often do you read the newspaper?	every day	once in a while	never
2. How often do you clean your room?	every day	once in a while	never
3. Do you study a lot?	every day	once in a while	never
4. Do you try to use new expressions when you speak English?	every day	once in a while	never
5. When you listen to people speak English, do you hear them using the new expressions?	every day	once in a while	never
6. How often do you _____?	every day	once in a while	never

2. whatéver you wánt = you can have or do anything that you want

- I had a crazy dream last night. I went to buy a car, and the salesperson said, "You can have **whatever you want** for just five dollars." So I bought a beautiful new car and then I woke up.

S1:   The party's at 8 o'clock.
S2:   Can I wear jeans?
S1:   You can wear **whatever you want.**

Similar Expressions: **wheréver you wánt** = in any place that you want
   whenéver you wánt = at any time that you want

S1:   Where do you want to eat?
S2:   **Wherever you want.**
S1:   Really? How about the new Chinese restaurant?

S1:   What time do you want to go?
S2:   **Whenever you want.**

Your Turn: Listening Challenge

As you listen to the tape, circle the letters of the correct answers.

1. (a) Whatever you want.   (b) Wherever you want.   (c) Whenever you want.

2. (a) Whatever you want.   (b) Wherever you want.   (c) Whenever you want.

3. (a) Whatever you want.   (b) Wherever you want.   (c) Whenever you want.

4. (a) Whatever you want.   (b) Wherever you want.   (c) Whenever you want.

5. (a) Whatever you want.   (b) Wherever you want.   (c) Whenever you want.

3. I'll háve = I would líke to órder. . . (I'd líke to órder. . .)

S1: Can I take your order?

S2: Yes. I think **I'll have** a ham and cheese omelette.

S1: With toast or a muffin?

S2: Toast. And my son **will have** scrambled eggs with toast.

S1: Anything to drink?

S2: Yes. **I'll have** coffee and **he'll have** orange juice.

Your Turn

The dialogue above is about ordering breakfast. Using that dialogue as an example, work with a partner and order lunch for yourself and your friend:

S1: Can I take your order?

S2: Yes. I_____.

S1: With soup or salad?

S2: _____. And my friend _____.

S1: Anything to drink?

S2: _____.

---

4. be húngry

Note: When you use this expression, be sure to use the verb *be.*

HUNGRY   ANGRY

Pronunciation Note: The *u* in *hungry* is pronounced like the *u* in the word *up.* The *a* in *angry* is pronounced like the *a* in the word *that.* Your jaw is low when you say "angry," and your jaw is higher when you say "hungry."

S1: Mom, I**'m hungry!**

S2: Well, dinner isn't ready. Here's a carrot for you.

S1: You ate a lot tonight.

S2: I know. I **was** very **hungry.**

Similar Expressions: **I'm stárving** = I'm very, very, very hungry.

I'm thírsty = I need something to drink.

● Let's get something to eat. **I'm starving** because I didn't have breakfast.

● Can you wait for me? I need to get some water because I**'m** very **thirsty.**

> **Your Turn:** Write a short dialogue. You are at school and you forgot your lunch. What do you say to your friend?
>
> **S1:** _____
>
> **S2:** _____

YES	NO

5. Are you réady to órder? = Can I táke your órder?

We're réady to órder.

S1: Hi. **Are you ready to order?** (Can I take your order?)

S2: Uh, I think we need a few more minutes to look at the menu.

S1: No problem. I'll come back in a few minutes.

> **Note:** You can call a waiter or waitress by saying, "We're ready to order." When you say this, you can try to catch the waiter or waitress' eye (look into his or her eye) and maybe raise your hand just a little bit. It is not polite to snap your fingers to get someone's attention.

S1: Excuse me. **We're ready to order.**

S2: I'll be right there.

All Clear?

Your Turn

How do you get the waiter's or waitress' attention in a restaurant in your native country?

____(a) wave your hand

____(b) catch his or her eye

____(c) snap your fingers

____(d) make a sound

____(e) other: _____

YES	NO

6. would like = want

Notes:
● "I would like. . ." is a polite way to say that you want something. It is more polite than saying "I want. . ." You can say "I would like" in a restaurant, in a person's home — anywhere.
● In a restaurant, when you order food, you can say "I would like" or "I'll have."

Pronunciation Note: *Would* is often used in contractions. These contractions are only one syllable:

I would = I'd like	we would = we'd like
you would = you'd like	they would = they'd like
he would = he'd like	
she would = she'd like	

Also, the *l* in *would* is silent. Don't say the *l*.

Question Form: **What would you like?** = What do you want? OR
Would you like. . .? = Do you want. . . ?

S1: Hi. Are you ready to order?
S2: Uh-huh. **I'd like** the fish special.
S1: And **what would you like?**
S3: I'll have the spaghetti.
S1: **Would you like** soup or salad with that?
S3: Salad. With oil and vinegar.

S1: **Would you like** more coffee?
S2: Sure. Thanks a lot.

YES	NO

7. for nów = for the moment (temporarily), but maybe later I will change something

S1:   Can I get you anything else?

S2:   No, thanks. I'm fine **for now.** (But maybe later I will want something else.)

S1:   Where do they live?

S2:   Well, **for now** they live in the city, but when they have children, they will move.

●   I know we have a lot to talk about, but **for now,** let's just talk about these expressions.

●   My car is OK **for now,** but I know that it is getting old.

●   This is enough **for now,** but maybe later we'll order dessert.

Your Turn: Finish these sentences:

1. I'm studying English for now, but later I will _____.

2. _____ is President of the U.S. for now, but later he (she?) will have to find another job.

3. _____ is my partner in class for now, but next week or next month I will have a new partner.

8. Hów about yóu? = And yóu?

S1: I'll have a turkey sandwich.
S2: And **how about you?** (And you?)
S3: I'd like a vegetarian burrito.

S1: What are you going to do this weekend?
S2: Nothing special. I'm going to stay home. Maybe I'll go to the movies. **How about you?** (And you?)
S1: I think I'll stay home, too. I have a lot of work to do.

Your Turn

Write a dialogue with *How about you?* and then read it with your partner.

S1: _____?
S2: _____. How about you?
S1: _____.

9. Will, thát be áll? = Is thát ít?
   Thát's áll. = Thát's ít.

Note: Notice the common answers to these questions.
A. Will that be all?   A. Is that it?
B. Yes, that's all.   B. Yes, that's it.

S1: OK. You want one hamburger, one cheeseburger, and two orders of fries. **Will that be all?** (Is that it?)
S2: Uh-huh. **That's all.** (That's it.)

Your Turn

Look at the Your Turn Section under number 6. Add to that dialogue with "Will that be all?" and "Yes, that's all."

Any Questions?

Take out a piece of paper. Do not write your name on it. On one side of the paper, write what you think is the most interesting information that you have learned in this lesson. On the other side of the paper, write any questions you have about what you studied or talked about in class. Your teacher will collect this paper and then answer your questions the next time you meet.

Exercises

1. Mini-Dialogues

Match the lines in A with the lines in B. You will then make mini-dialogues.

To check this exercise, say each mini-dialogue with a partner. One student will read a line from A, and another student will answer with a line from B.

1. A

____1. Are you ready to order?
____2. How often do you eat here?
____3. Where do you want to eat?
____4. When do want to leave?
____5. Can I get you anything else?

1. B

a. Wherever you want.
b. Not yet. We need another minute.
c. Whenever you want.
d. No, thanks. I'm fine for now.
e. Once in a while.

2. A

____1. What are you going to have?
____2. Would you like some more coffee?
____3. Will that be all?
____4. Dad, what kind of drink can I get?
____5. I'm so thirsty.

2. B

a. No, thanks. I'm fine.
b. Yes, that's all.
c. Whatever you want.
d. Why don't you ask for some water?
e. I'm not very hungry. I think I'll just have a cup of soup.

2. Scene Two — Listening

The following is a conversation between the brother and sister in the introductory dialogue. Now it is about six months later, and the sister is taking her brother to lunch for his birthday.

As you listen to the tape, fill in the blanks with the expressions that you hear. Be sure to use a capital letter at the beginning of a sentence. When you finish, perform the dialogue with two other students.

Are You Ready to Order?

BROTHER:	Now I can thank you. I think going out to lunch is a great birthday present.
SISTER:	Well, I'm just glad to have time to sit and talk with you. Life these days is so busy. . .
WAITER:	Hi! (1) _____?
SISTER:	I'm sorry. We need a few more minutes.
WAITER:	No problem. I'll come back.
BROTHER:	So, what are you going to have?
SISTER:	I don't know, but I want you to order (2) _____.
BROTHER:	I have to tell you, I (3) _____. . .
SISTER:	That's OK. It's your birthday and you can have anything. Hmm. . . I think (4) _____the fish special. It sounds really good.
BROTHER:	You know, I think (5) _____ the same thing.
SISTER:	Where's the waiter? . . . Oh, there he is. . . Excuse me. (6) _____.
WAITER:	(7) _____?
SISTER:	(8) _____ the fish special.
WAITER:	With soup or salad?
SISTER:	Salad. With oil and vinegar on the side, please.
WAITER:	And (9) _____?
BROTHER:	I'll have the same.
WAITER:	OK. That's two fish specials and two salads with oil and vinegar on the side. (10) _____?
SISTER:	Yes, that's all (11) _____. Thanks.

3. Dictation

Your teacher or one of your classmates will read the dictation for this lesson from Appendix C, or you will listen to the dictation on the tape. You will hear the dictation three times. First, just listen. Second, as you listen, write the dictation on a separate sheet of paper. Third, as you listen, check what you have written.

period .
comma ,
apostrophe '
question mark ?

Proofread

● Does every sentence start with a capital letter?

● Do the sentences end with a period or question mark?

FOR THIS DICTATION, YOU WILL HEAR A DIALOGUE. Before you start, write the following on the left side of your paper:

Waitress:

Customer:

Waitress:

Customer:

Waitress:

Customer:

Waitress:

Customer:

Check yourself

After you check your dictation, look at your mistakes. What do you have to be more careful about next time?

___spelling	___vocabulary
___plurals	___verb tenses
___subject-verb agreement	___punctuation

Other: _____

4. Pronunciation — Stress & Intonation

1. Review the rules about stress (Lesson 3) and intonation (Lesson 4).
2. Below is the beginning of the introductory dialogue from this lesson. As you say the dialogue with a partner, do the following:

● Stress the capitalized words—make them longer, stronger, and louder than other words.

● Make your voice go up and down the way the words appear. Try to read with feeling.

SISTER: Oh, this is so NICE. What a great BIRTHday present!

BROTHER: I'm glad you LIKE it. I was THINKing, you KNOW, we never really

have TIME to just SIT and TALK. . .

SISTER: And now we have two HOURS! And this is a really nice PLACE.

BROTHER: Yeah, I come here ONCE in a while.

SISTER: What are you going to HAVE?

BROTHER: Um. . . I'm not SURE yet. But YOU order whatEVER you WANT.

It's your BIRTHday.

3. Listen to the tape of this dialogue. Notice which words are stressed and how the speakers' voices go up and down.
4. With a partner, perform the whole dialogue between the brother and sister. Give special attention to stress and intonation.
5. Listen to the tape of the restaurant dialogue in Exercise 2. Then perform that dialogue with two partners.

5. Walk & Talk — Find Someone Who

1) Walk around the room and ask about five of your classmates the following questions: What is your favorite kind of appetizer? soup? salad? main course? dessert? beverage?

Write short answers in the chart. You don't need to write students' names.

Favorite Kinds of				
Appetizers	**Soups and Salads**	**Main Courses**	**Desserts**	**Beverages**

2) After you get the information, get into a group of three or four students. Imagine that you are all going to open a new international restaurant together. Give your restaurant a name, and use the information in the chart above to make a menu. Add to the menu if you want. Decide on the prices you will charge.

(name of restaurant)

Appetizers	$	**Soups**	$
●		●	
●		●	
●		●	
●		●	
●		●	

Salads	$	**Main Courses**	$
●		● Today's Special: _____	
●		●	
●		●	
●		●	
●		●	

Desserts	$	**Beverages**	$
●		●	
●		●	
●		●	
●		●	
●		●	

6. Write

Alone or with a partner, write a paragraph about the restaurant that your group will open. Give the name of the restaurant and talk about some of the kinds of food that you will serve. Also, give the price range of the main courses (for example, main courses cost from $3 to $10). (Use the future tense.)

We will open an international restaurant. We will name the restaurant

_____

_____

_____

_____

_____

_____

7. Role Play

Choose three or four of students to open a restaurant. They will be waiters and waitresses. They will each have four copies of the menus they made in Exercise 5.

Do the following:

● On the board, write: the name of the restaurant
expressions listed in Exercise 10

● Choose three or four groups of students to each sit at a group of desks. These will be the tables at the restaurant. (If there are more students in the class, they can join the tables or listen and watch.)

- The waiters and waitresses will each have a table to serve. They will give menus to the customers. The customers will order lunch or dinner.

- Try to use as many of the new expressions as possible. If you can, bring in tablecloths, cups, plates, etc.

Possible first lines: How are you today? Here are the menus. I'll be back in a few minutes to take your order.

Possible way to end: Excuse me. Can we have the check, please?

8. Tic-Tac-Toe — Play & Write

In tic-tac-toe, to get an *X* or an *O* in a space, you need to make a sentence that is correct in grammar and meaning. Here is a game with expressions from Lesson 5. (See page 15 for more detailed directions.)

once in a while	for now	whatever you want
I would like	Would you like __?	wherever you want
whenever you want	I'll have	be thirsty

After you play tic-tac-toe, write sentences using all of the expressions. When you write, start every sentence with a capital letter, think about spelling, and be careful with verb tenses and other grammar that you are studying.

9. Expression Clusters & Charts

1. Add expressions from this lesson to the expression clusters in Appendix D.
2. When you hear or read expressions that you have studied in class, add them to Appendix E.
3. Write down new expressions from outside of class in Appendix F.

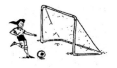

10. Goal Post

Can you now use the new expressions when you listen and speak? Put (a) or (b) next to each expression in the chart below:

	For Listening	For Speaking
	(a) I know what this expression means. (b) I'm not sure what this expression means.	(a) I am comfortable saying this when I speak. (b) I am not comfortable saying this when I speak.
once in awhile	_____	_____
for now	_____	_____
whatever you want	_____	_____
wherever you want	_____	_____
whenever you want	_____	_____
I'll have ____	_____	_____
I'd like ____	_____	_____
be hungry	_____	_____
be thirsty	_____	_____
Are you ready to order?	_____	X*
Can I take your order?	_____	X*
We're ready to order.	_____	_____
Will that be all?	_____	X*
That's all	_____	_____
Is that it?	_____	X*
That's it.	_____	_____

	For Listening	**For Speaking**
	(a) I know what this expression means.	(a) I am comfortable saying this when I speak.
	(b) I'm not sure what this expression means.	(b) I am not comfortable saying this when I speak.
What would you like?	_____	_____
Would you like?	_____	_____
How about you?	_____	_____
And you?	_____	_____

*The X shows that this is something that a waiter or waitress asks in a restaurant.

If you gave any expression a (b), be sure to ask your teacher or a classmate for help.

Before you start the next lesson, answer these questions about this lesson:

● What did you do to learn new expressions?

● What activities helped you the most?

Lesson 6 My Leg Is Killing Me!

Talking About Your Health

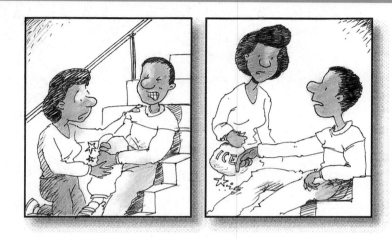

Warm-Up

1. Did you ever break a bone? If yes, what happened? Who helped you?
2. When people get hurt and feel pain, they often say "Ow!" or "Ouch!" What sound do people make in your native language when they get hurt?

    English: Ow! or Ouch!
    Your native language: _____

Focused Listening

BEFORE YOU LISTEN

● Look at the cartoon. Write down what you think is happening.

         Picture 1   **Picture 2**

a. Mike _____   d. Judy _____

b. Mike feels _____   e. Mike's leg _____

c. Judy _____

● What do you think Mike and Judy will do? _____

AS YOU LISTEN

Listen to the dialogue to see if what you wrote under Before You Listen is correct.

AFTER YOU LISTEN

- Make changes in the Before You Listen exercise if necessary.
- Listen to the tape again, but this time, listen while you read the dialogue below.
- Say the dialogue with a partner.
- Have two volunteers perform the dialogue in front of the class.

MIKE: Ow. My leg **is killing me.**

JUDY: **What happened?**

MIKE: I **fell down** the stairs.

JUDY: Do you think it's broken?

MIKE: I don't know, but **it hurts** a lot.

JUDY: Maybe you need to go to the emergency room.

MIKE: Oh, let's wait a few minutes and see if it gets better.

JUDY: OK. But can I get you anything?

MIKE: Hmm. . . Maybe some ice.

JUDY: OK. I'll **be right back**. . . OK, here. Can you move your leg?

MIKE: **I think so.** But look — it's **getting swollen.**

JUDY: Listen, I'm taking you to the hospital **right away. Stay put** and don't move. I'm going to get the car.

Understanding the New Expressions

Learn with Others and/or On Your Own

WITH OTHERS

Work with a partner or in a small group.

ON YOUR OWN

Work on this section carefully. For each expression, put an X in the *Yes* or *No* box in the margin to show if you understand the information.

(For more detailed directions, see page 3.)

All Clear?

YES	NO

1. be killing someone

> **Note:** You say this when a part of your body hurts very, very much. It does not mean that anyone is being killed.

S1: My head is **killing me.**
S2: Why don't you take some aspirin?
S1: I don't have any. Do you?
S2: Uh-huh. Here. Take two. I'll get you some water.
S1: Thanks a lot.

S1: Where's Rick?
S2: His tooth is **killing him,** so he went to the dentist.
S1: I hope he's OK.
S2: So do I.

> **Your Turn**
>
> Complain to your partner that something really hurts. Your partner will try to help you by giving you ideas about how you can get better.
>
> You: Oh, my _____ is killing me.
>
> Your partner: Why don't you _____?

YES	NO

2. What happened?

> **Pronunciation Note:** Don't add a new syllable to the word *happen* when you add *ed.* Pronounce *happened* as "happend."

Uh-oh = Oh, no. Something is wrong.

S1: **What happened?**
S2: I can't find my wallet.
S1: Uh-oh. Let me help you look for it.

All Clear?

S1: I was absent this morning. Can you tell me **what happened** in class?

S2: Sure. We worked in groups and then we had a quiz.

> **Your Turn**
>
> Ask another student to tell you what happened in class yesterday or last week. Make a list.

3. fall dówn   (past = fell)

> **Notes:**
>
> ● Usually we don't put words after "fall down." Usually we just say "I fell down." But we can say *where* we fell down: "I fell down the stairs." We can also say "I fell down *and* broke my leg."
>
> ● Be careful with the past tense. The past of *fall* is *fell*. The past of *feel* is *felt*.

S1: Why is he crying?

S2: He **fell down** and hurt his knee.

● There's ice on the ground, and you need to be careful or you'll **fall down**.

Similar Expressions: **fall óff** (something) /**fall óut** (of something)

> **Note:** If something is ON something like a table, it can FALL OFF.
> If something is IN something like a pocket, it can FALL OUT (OF SOMETHING).

● The book was on the table. When the earthquake hit, the book **fell off** (the table).

● His keys were in his pocket. When he was walking, his keys **fell out** (of his pocket).

S1: What happened during the earthquake?

S2: I stayed under a table and things **fell off** bookshelves and they **fell out of** kitchen cabinets. I was scared.

Your Turn

Fill in the blanks with *fell off, fell out of,* or *fell down.* All of these sentences are in the past tense.

During the earthquake,

1. The plate was ON the table.   it fell OFF the table.

2. The picture was ON the wall.   it _____ the wall.

3. The book was ON the shelf.   it _____ the shelf.

4. Your example:

   _____   _____

When she was running,

5. Her keys were IN her pocket.   her keys _____
                                   her pocket.

6. A book was IN her backpack.   a book _____
                                   her backpack.

7. Her wallet was IN her purse.   her wallet _____
                                   her purse.

8. Your example:

   _____   _____

9. The ice skater _____ three times last night. Ouch!

10. The baby _____ a lot when he was learning to walk.

11. During the earthquake, many people _____.

12. Your example: _____

4. will be right back = will return immediately

S1: Oh, I forgot my wallet. **I'll be right back.**
S2: I'll wait here.

S1: Where's Judy?
S2: She went to get some ice. **She'll be right back.**

> **Your Turn:**   Complete these dialogues—
> **S1:** Where's _____?
> **S2:** He'll be right back. He _____.
>
> **S1:** Where are _____?
> **S2:** They'll be right back. They _____.

5. I think so.

> **Note:**   This can be an answer to a yes-no question. *I think so* means "I think yes, but I'm not 100% sure."

> **Pronunciation Note:**   Practice saying the voiceless "th" sound when you say "I think so." To make the sound, put your tongue between your front teeth and blow air. Put your hand in front of your mouth to feel the air. Don't be afraid to have your tongue out a little bit. If your tongue is in, you will make the /t/ or /s/ sound, not the "th."

S1: Is she sleeping?
S2: **I think so.** I'll go check. . . Yes, she's asleep. (or: No, she's awake.)

S1: Do we have a test today?
S2: **I think so.** . . Let me see. . . Uh-huh. That's right. The teacher said Tuesday.

Opposite: **I don't think so.**

S1: Is his leg broken?
S2: **I don't think so,** but he needs to have an X ray so we can be sure.

S1: Are they coming to the party tonight?
S2: **I don't think so.** They said they were probably going to stay home.

> **Note:**   You can say "Yes, I think so" or "No, I don't think so" when you answer the question "Do you think. . ." and give your *opinion:*

S1: Do you think we should leave early?
S2: Yeah, **I think so.** There's going to be a lot of traffic.

S1: Do you think English is easy?
S2: No, **I don't think so.**

Your Turn: Ask your partner the following questions. Your partner will answer with "I think so" or "I don't think so."

Question	Answer
1. Do you think Judy is Mike's mother?	_____
2. Do you think Mike has a broken leg?	_____
3. Did Mike and Judy go to the hospital?	_____
4. Did Mike go to work the next day?	_____
5. Do you think Mike will be more careful on the stairs next time?	_____

YES	NO

6. it húrts   (past = hurt)

Note: You can say something *hurts* when you feel pain in parts of your body.

S1: How's your leg?
S2: **It hurts** a lot, so I can't walk.

S1: You look better today. How's your leg?
S2: Thanks. **It hurt** a lot yesterday, but today I'm feeling better.

Pronunciation Note:
* *Ache* is pronounced "ayk."
* Stress the first word in "noun compounds." (The stressed parts of the words are in capital letters.)

My head		I have a HEADache.
My stomach		I have a STOMACHache.
My tooth	hurts.	I have a TOOTHache.
My back		I have a BACKache.
My ear		I have an EARache.

Your Turn: Listening Challenge

The person on the tape is complaining. He has a lot of problems. Tell him what to do to feel better.

Your Advice:

1. You should _____.
2. You should _____.
3. You should _____.
4. You should _____.
5. You should _____.

7. gét/be swóllen

> **Note:** When a part of the body gets bigger because you get hurt or because you break a bone, it gets "swollen."

S1: How's your leg, Mike?
S2: **It's getting swollen.** I think I need some ice.

S1: How's your leg now, Mike?
S2: It hurts and **it's swollen.** I think I need to see a doctor.

S1: How's your leg now, Mike?
S2: It's much better. It **was swollen** yesterday, but today it's better.

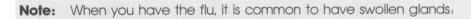

> **Note:** When you have the flu, it is common to have swollen glands.

S1: What's wrong? You look sick.
S2: I am. **I have swollen glands** and a sore throat.

Your Turn: These are problems when you have a cold or have the flu:

When you have a cold, you:

sneeze
cough (*gh* is pronounced
  like an *f*)

When you have the flu, you can:

have a fever
sneeze
cough
have a sore throat
have swollen glands
have an upset stomach

Talk about the last time you had a cold or the flu. How did you feel?
What medicine did you take?

8. ríght awáy = immediately

S1: Mom, can you come home? I feel sick.
S2: What's wrong?
S1: I have a sore throat, and I think I have a fever.
S2: I'll be there **right away.**

S1: Is dinner ready? I'm hungry.
S2: It'll be ready **right away.** Why don't you set the table?

Your Turn: Complete these three dialogues.

(a) Mother: _____.
   Child: I'll be there right away.

(b) Child: _____.
   Mother: I'll be there right away.

(c) Person: _____.
   Police: We'll be there right away.

9. stáy pút = stay where you are; don't go anywhere

MY MOM TOLD ME TO STAY PUT.

S1: I need to go to work.

S2: No, you don't. You have the flu. Just **stay put** and don't go anywhere. Take care of yourself.

● We moved two times in five years. I don't want to move anymore. I want to stay put.

> **Your Turn:** Complete this dialogue. There is a big storm outside. What does Speaker B say to Speaker A?
>
> A: Let's go to the movies.
>
> B: _____.

Any Questions?

Take out a piece of paper. Do not write your name on it. On one side of the paper, write what you think is the most interesting information that you have learned in this lesson. On the other side of the paper, write any questions you have about what you studied or talked about in class. Your teacher will collect this paper and then answer your questions the next time you meet.

Exercises

1. Mini-Dialogues

Match the lines in A with the lines in B. You will then make mini-dialogues.

To check this exercise, say each mini-dialogue with a partner. One student will read a line from A, and another student will answer with a line from B.

> Nope is a friendly way to say "no."

1. A

____1. Mama! I fell down! Aah!

____2. Are you going anywhere this weekend?

____3. Oh, my hand is killing me.

____4. Are Judy and Mike married?

____5. What happened to Mike?

1. B

a. Nope. We're going to stay put and relax at home.

b. I think so, but I'm not sure.

c. He fell down the stairs and broke his leg.

d. Maybe you're working at your computer too much.

e. Come over here and let me look at your knee.

2. B

____1. Where are you going? We have to leave right away.

____2. Look! My wrist is getting swollen.

____3. My favorite cup fell off the table and broke.

____4. What happened? Why are you on crutches?

____5. Do you think it's going to snow?

2. B

a. I'll be right back. Don't worry.

b. I broke my leg.

c. I'll get you another one.

d. You're right. Do you think you broke it?

e. No, I don't think so. It's not cold enough.

2. Scene Two — Listening

The following is a conversation between Mike and Judy. They are at a hospital emergency room.

As you listen to the tape, fill in the blanks with the expressions that you hear. Be sure to use a capital letter at the beginning of a sentence. When you finish, perform the dialogue with two other students.

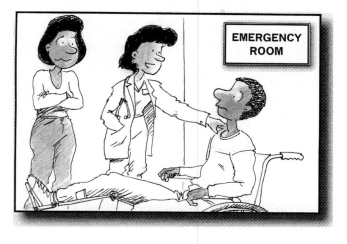

DR. GREEN:	Hi, I'm Dr. Green. What can I do for you today?
MIKE:	My leg (1) _____. I think I broke it.
DR. GREEN:	(2) _____?
MIKE:	I (3) _____ the stairs. I was reading something and I wasn't paying attention. . .
DR. GREEN:	Hmm. That's how these things happen. Here, let me take a look. . . Well, your leg (4) _____.
MIKE:	And I put ice on it.
DR. GREEN:	You need to get an X ray (5) _____. Wait here a moment and (6) _____.
	(a few minutes later)
DR. GREEN:	Excuse me, what's your name?
JUDY:	Judy.
DR. GREEN:	OK, Judy, take Mike down the hall to room 212 for his X ray. Then go back to the waiting room and I'll call you.
JUDY:	Thanks, Dr. Green. Do you think his leg's broken?
DR. GREEN:	(7) _____, but I want to be sure.
JUDY:	OK. Thanks, doctor. Let's go, Mike.

My Leg Is Killing Me!

period .
comma ,
apostrophe '

3. Dictation

Your teacher or one of your classmates will read the dictation for this lesson from Appendix C, or you will listen to the dictation on the tape. You will hear the dictation three times. First, just listen. Second, as you listen, write the dictation on a separate sheet of paper. Third, as you listen, check what you have written.

Proofread

- Did you indent the first line of each paragraph?
- Does every sentence start with a capital letter?
- Do the names have capital letters?
- Do the sentences end with a period?

Check yourself

After you check your dictation, look at your mistakes. What do you have to be more careful about next time?

____spelling   ____vocabulary

____plurals   ____verb tenses

____subject-verb agreement   ____punctuation

Other: _____

4. Pronunciation — Question Intonation

Here are the questions from this lesson's two dialogues:

Yes-No Questions	**Information (WH) Questions**
Do you think it's broken?	What happened?
Can I get you anything?	What can I do for you today?
Can you move your leg?	What's your name?
Do you think his leg's broken?	

Yes-No Questions — Rising Intonation

When you ask a yes-no question, remember that your voice needs to rise (go up) at the end of the question. (See Lesson 4.) Practice asking the questions below:

1) Do you think it's bro ken?

2) Can I get you any thing?

3) Can you move your leg?

4) Do you think his leg's bro ken?

When you ask an information question, remember that your voice needs to rise (go up) on the last stressed word, and then fall (go down) at the end of the question. Practice asking the questions below:

> If the last stressed word is one syllable, you have to stretch it out (make it longer).

1) What happened?

2) What can I do for you today?

3) What's your name?

PRONUNCIATION & LISTENING PRACTICE

● These are the questions from the introductory dialogue in Lesson 5. Practice asking these questions, using the rules for question intonation:

Yes-No Questions	**Information Questions**
Example: Are you ready to order? (Do you want) anything to drink? Will that be all?	What are you going to have? How about you?

● Listen to the tape of the introductory dialogues in Lessons 5 and 6, and pay special attention to the intonation used in questions. Then practice repeating these questions as you listen to the tape.

● Do the Hot Seat activity in Appendix K. As you ask questions, think about question intonation.

5. Walk & Talk Jigsaw

(a) Get into groups of three or four. You are Student 1.

● Under Student 1, write your first name and your own answers to the two questions. Your answers can be very short. You don't need to write sentences.

● Ask members of your group the same questions. Complete this chart with information from students 2, 3, and 4. (Be sure to *talk* to people in your group—don't read to each other.)

Questions	Student 1	Student 2	Student 3	Student 4	Information from Traveling Students
1. What do you do to feel better when you have a cold or the flu?					
2. In your native country, what do (or did) your parents or grandparents do for a cold or the flu?					

(b) After you complete the chart for students 1, 2, 3, and 4, send one or two students to another group. These are the "traveling students." (Every new group will still have three or four students.)

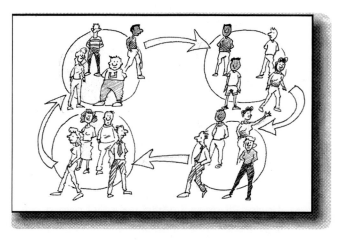

- The traveling students will talk to the members of the group they are visiting. The "travelers" will explain how students in their first group answered the two questions. (Traveler 1 can explain Question 1; Traveler 2 can explain Question 2.) The students who are not "travelers" can write new information in the chart under "Information from Traveling Students."

- After a few minutes, the traveling students will move to another group and give the same information. The traveling students will continue to travel until they return to their original "home" group.

(c) When the traveling students return "home" to their first group, the "home" group will look at their notes and tell the travelers the new information they got from other travelers.

(d) The class can make a list on the board of all the things people do (or did) when they have a cold or the flu.

6. Write

Write sentences about what three students told you in Exercise 5. After you finish, you can show the sentences to those students to make sure that your information is correct.

- _____

- _____

- _____

7. Role Play

Imagine that your classroom is a doctor's office. Choose students for the following roles:

- doctor

- nurse

- receptionist

- four adult patients

- one mother or father with a child

The five patients all have different problems:

- Mike has a broken leg (Judy may be with him.)

- someone has the flu (with fever, coughing, sneezing, sore throat, swollen glands)

- someone has a cold (with sneezing and coughing)

- someone has a stomachache

- the child has an earache (his or her parent is very worried)

Each patient comes in one at a time and goes to the receptionist. The receptionist gets the person's name and asks the patient to sit down or "take a seat." Then the receptionist gives the list of names to the nurse.

After all of the patients are sitting in the waiting room, the nurse comes out and asks for the first patient. Each patient goes in to see the doctor and nurse and tells them what the problem is. When they finish, they leave and the next patient goes in. The doctor and nurse ask a lot of questions and help the patients.

Here are some expressions that you can try to use. They can be written on the board.

_____ is killing me	I fell down
have swollen glands	I think so
get/be swollen	I don't think so
right away	have a cold
have a _____ache	have the flu
have a fever	have a sore throat

Possible starting lines:

Receptionist. Hi. Can I help you?

Patient: Yes, I have an appointment with Dr. _____.

Receptionist: What's your name?

Patient: _____

Receptionist: OK. Please have a seat.

8. Tic-Tac-Toe — Play & Write

In tic-tac-toe, to get an *X* or an *O* in a space, you need to make a sentence that is correct in grammar and meaning. Here is a game with expressions from Lesson 6. (See page 15 for more detailed directions.)

fall down	fall off	fall out of
right away	stay put	____ hurts
is swollen	will be right back	____ is killing me because

After you play tic-tac-toe, write sentences using all of the expressions. When you write, start every sentence with a capital letter, think about spelling, and be careful with verb tenses and other grammar that you are studying.

9. Expression Clusters & Charts

1. Add expressions from this lesson to the expression clusters in Appendix D.
2. When you hear or read expressions that you have studied in class, add them to Appendix E.
3. Write down new expressions from outside of class in Appendix F.

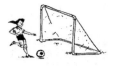

10. Goal Post

Can you now use the new expressions when you listen and speak? Put (a) or (b) next to each expression in the chart below:

	For Listening (a) I know what this expression means. (b) I'm not sure what this expression means.	**For Speaking** (a) I am comfortable saying this when I speak. (b) I am not comfortable saying this when I speak.
is killing me	_____	_____
What happened?	_____	_____
fall down	_____	_____
fall out of	_____	_____
fall off	_____	_____
it hurts	_____	_____
will be right back	_____	_____
I think so	_____	_____
I don't think so	_____	_____
get/be swollen	_____	_____
right away	_____	_____
stay put	_____	_____
have a cold	_____	_____
have the flu	_____	_____
have a(n) __ache	_____	_____

If you gave any expression a (b), be sure to ask your teacher or a classmate for help.

Before you start the next lesson, answer these questions about this lesson:

● What did you do to learn new expressions?

● What activities helped you the most?

Crossword Puzzle for Lessons 5 and 6

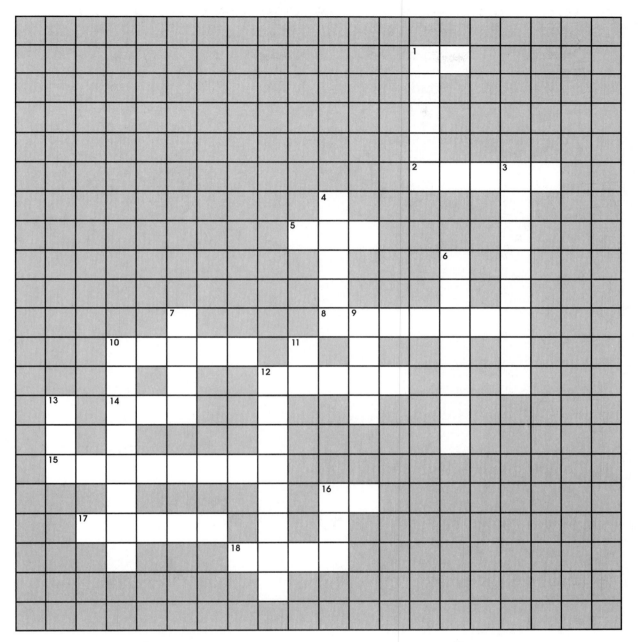

Across

1. My book fell out ___ my backpack.
2. I'm coming ___ away.
5. Stay ___. Don't go anywhere.
8. I feel sick and my glands are ___.
10. We go to the movies once in a ___.

Down

1. Can I take your ___?
3. What ___?
4. I had a shot (injection) and my arm ___.
6. My head is ___ me.
7. I'd ___ a salad.

Across

12. What ___ you like?
14. We ___ very hungry tonight.
15. You can go there ___ you want.
16. I ___ really thirsty. Can I have some water?
17. Excuse me. We're ___ to order.
18. I ___ down when I was skiing.

Down

9. ___ that be all?
10. You can do ___ you want.
11. I don't think ___.
12. You can go ___ you want.
13. We're fine for ___.
16. That's ___.

Lesson 7 Shopping for Jeans

Shopping and Giving Compliments

Warm-Up

In one minute, write words about shopping in the empty circles. Then share what you wrote with a partner or your class.

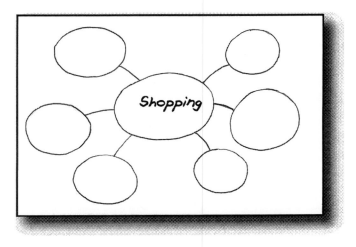

Focused Listening

● Look at the cartoon and read these sentences. *Don't write the answers now.*

____1. The salesclerk wants to help Jim.

____2. Jim wants to buy jeans.

____3. The salesclerk says the jeans are very expensive.

____3. Jim tries jeans that are too small.

____4. Lynn finds better jeans for Jim.

____5. Jim buys a nice pair of jeans.

AS YOU LISTEN

Listen to find out which of the five sentences are True or False.

T	F	?

AFTER YOU LISTEN

● Complete the Before You Listen exercise. On the lines on the left, write **T** for sentences that are true, **F** for sentences that are false and **?** for sentences that you are not sure about. Check your answers with a partner.

● Listen to the tape again, but this time, listen while you read the dialogue on the next page.

● Say the dialogue in groups of three.

● Have three volunteers perform the dialogue in front of the class.

SALESCLERK:	Can I help you?
LYNN:	Thanks, **we're just looking.**
SALESCLERK:	Well, **let me know** if there's anything I can do for you.

❖ ❖ ❖ ❖ ❖

JIM:	**What do you think of** these jeans?
LYNN:	They're really nice. **How much** are they?
JIM:	Hmm. . . there's no price tag. Where's the salesperson? I'm going to ask her. . . Oh, there she is. Excuse me, **how much** are these jeans?
SALESCLERK:	I'll be with you in a minute. . . . OK. Let's see. They were $29, but I think today they're 30 percent off. Yes, that's right. They're about $20. That's a good price for such nice jeans.
JIM:	Can I **try them on?**
SALESCLERK:	Sure. The fitting rooms are right **over there.** Just **go on in.**
JIM:	Thanks a lot.

❖ ❖ ❖ ❖ ❖

JIM:	Pssst. Lynn, how do they look?
LYNN:	Oh, Jim! They're too big. I'll get you a smaller size. . . Wait a minute . . . Here, try these.
JIM:	Thanks. . . Yeah, I think these are better. How do they look?
LYNN:	Fine.
SALESCLERK:	Oh, they look very nice on you.
JIM:	Great. **I'll take** them.

■ Understanding the New Expressions

Learn with Others and/or On Your Own

WITH OTHERS

Work with a partner or in a small group.

ON YOUR OWN

Work on this section carefully, and then for each expression put an X in the *Yes* or *No* box in the margin to show if you understand the information.

(For more detailed directions, see pages 3–4.)

1. I'm júst lóoking./We're júst lóoking.

> **Note:** You can say this to a salesperson if you don't want help when you are shopping.

S1: Hi. Can I help you?
S2: Thanks. **I'm just looking.** (We're just looking.)
S1: Fine. Let me know if you need any help.
S2: I will.

> **Your Turn:** Say the dialogue above with a partner.

2. lét (me, you, him, her, us, them) knów = tell (me) later

> **Grammar Note:** This expression is usually in two forms:
> ● imperative (command): (Please) let me know!
> ● future tense: I'll let you know (later).
>
> **Pronunciation Note:** The last sound in I'll is l and the first sound in let
> is l. When you say, "I'll let you know," pronounce I'll let as one word.

S1: Did she have a girl or a boy?
S2: I don't know. I'm going to call them right now.
S1: Please **let me know** as soon as you can.
S2: I'll call you right away.

S1: This homework is really hard.
S2: **Let me know** if you need my help.

S1: Do you want to go shopping tomorrow?
S2: I'm not sure yet. I'll **let you know** tonight.

S1: They need to know where the party is.
S2: I'll **let them know.**

> **Your Turn:** Finish the sentences on the right.
>
> 1. I need to know what time   I'll let you know later.
>   the movie starts.
> 2. They want to know if they   The teacher will _____
>   passed the test.
> 3. When is the party?   I _____
> 4. Can you come on Friday night?   I'm not sure. _____

3. Whát do you thínk of . . . ? = Whát is your opínion of . . . ?

S1: **What do you think of** classical music?
S2: I like it a lot. But I like rock music better.

S1: **What do you think of** this watch?
S2: It's nice, but it's too expensive.

S1: **What do you think of** American food?
S2: Hmm. That's a difficult question.

Your Turn: Ask your partner for his or her opinion.

Question		Answer (use adjectives)
What do you think of	American food?	I think it's _____
	English?	_____
	classical music?	_____
	rock music?	_____
	_____	_____
	_____	_____

4. How much are they?/How much is this?

Grammar Note: Say "How much are they?" if you are asking about a plural noun; use "How much is this?" if you are asking about a singular or uncountable noun.

- These shoes are nice.   **How much are they?**
- Those are nice pants.

- That's a nice watch.   **How much is it?**
- I like that jacket.

Your Turn: On the left is a list of things in a department store. On the right, write what question you can ask to get the price. Use *it* or *they*.

Things to Buy	Question
1. table	How much _____?
2. earrings	_____
3. boots	_____
4. sweater	_____
5. T-shirt	_____
6. sunglasses	_____
7. _____	_____

5. try (something) ón = put on clothes or shoes to see if they fit (if they are the right size) and to see if they look nice

S1: Excuse me. Can I **try this on?**
S2: Sure. The fitting room is over there.

S1: Where's Jim?
S2: He's **trying** some jeans **on.**

Grammar Note: It is common to use IT (singular) or THEM (plural) with this two-word verb.

When you use *it* and *them,* be sure to put them in the middle:

This is a nice shirt. Where can I **try it on?**

My shoes hurt. They didn't hurt yesterday when I **tried them on.**

Grammar Notes About Singular & Plural:
● Think of *shorts, pants,* and *jeans* as plural nouns (for two legs).
● *This* and *that* are used with singular nouns, and *these* and *those* are used with plural nouns. *This* and *these* are used with things that are close to you, and *that* and *those* are used with things that are not near you.

	SINGULAR	**PLURAL**
	it	them
NEAR	this	these
FAR	that	those

Grammar Notes about when to use IT or THIS:
● Both IT and THIS can be used for singular and uncountable nouns.
● Use IT when you already said the word that IT refers to. For example:

I like this sweater. Where can I try IT on?
("this sweater" = IT)

● Use THIS when you and the person you are talking to both *see* what you want to try on. For example:

Excuse me. Where can I try THIS on?
(You don't say the word "sweater," but you and the salesclerk know what you mean when you say the word THIS because you are holding the sweater and you both see it.)

Your Turn: Listening Challenge

Listen to the tape and fill in the blanks with *it* or *them.*

1. Where can I try _____ on?

2. I'm going to try _____ on.

3. Why didn't I try _____ on before I bought it?

4. You do? Here, try _____ on.

5. Uh-huh. I tried _____ on.

YES	NO

6. over thére

Notes:
● It is common to say "right over there" and "go over there." "There" is not near you.
● Use the word *come* with "here" and *go* with "there."

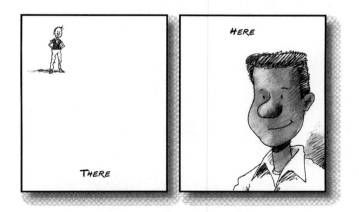

S1: Excuse me. Where's the teacher?
S2: She's **right over there.**
S1: Oh, I see her. Thanks.

S1: Where is my book?
S2: I think it's at Lynn's house. Didn't you leave it there yesterday?

All Clear?

S1: Oh, that's right! I need to **go over there** and get it because I need to do my homework.

S2: Do you want me to come with you?

Similar Expression: **over hére**

S1: Where are you?

S2: I'm **over here.** Under the car.

S1: Dad, I fell and my leg hurts.

S2: Come **over here** and let me look at it.

Your Turn: On the right, write *over there* or *over here*.

1. He's with me.   He's _____.

2. He's across the street. He's _____.

---

7. gó on ín

Note: This is a friendly way to tell someone to go into something that is "over there."

S1: Is the restaurant open?

S2: Uh-huh. **Go on in.**

S1: Don't wait for me. I'll park the car. You **go on in.**

S2: OK. We'll see you inside.

Similar Expression: **Cóme on ín** = friendly way to say "Come in."

Note: You can say "Come on in" when you want someone to come into a place where you are. You can say "Go on in" when you want someone to go into a place, but you are not there.

S1: Hi, you guys! **Come on in.** It's great to see you!

S2: Thanks. It's great to be here.

Your Turn: On the right, write *come on in* or *go on in*.

1. I'll be right there. Don't wait for me. _____.

2. Welcome! _____.

8. Hów do they lóok?/Hów does it lóok?
They look.../It looks... (+ adjective)

Note: You can ask people these questions when you try clothes on. You ask these questions if you want their opinion. They will tell you if the clothes "look good on you."

S1: What do you think of these shoes? **How do they look?**

S2: **They look** really nice. Are they comfortable?

S1: What do you think of this jacket? **How does it look?**

S2: I think it's too long.

Note: *Look like* is a different expression. It means "resemble," and it is followed by a noun. For example, "you *look like* your father."

Your Turn: Get an advertisement with a picture from a magazine or newspaper. Write down at least three things the person or people are wearing in the ad. Then write a question and answer for each item.

What They Are Wearing	Question	Answer (use adjectives)
Example: a necklace	How does it look?	It looks beautiful.
earrings	How do they look?	They look beautiful.
_____	_____	_____
_____	_____	_____
_____	_____	_____
_____	_____	_____

9. I'll (We'll) táke ____.

Note: You can say this to a salesclerk in a store when you are ready to buy something.

S1:	Hi. Do you want to take this sweater?
S2:	Yes. **I'll take it.**

S1:	Hi. We're ready. **We'll take** this chair.
S2:	OK. I'll be right with you.

S1:	Hi. **I'll take** these jeans.
S2:	Will that be all? (Do you want anything else?)
S1:	Yes, that's all.

Your Turn: This can be done as a whole class or in groups. Put some items (books, pens, wallets, purses, earrings, jackets, etc.) on a desk in your classroom. One student can be the salesclerk and another person can be a customer. Think about singular and plural, and follow this sample dialogue:

S1:	Can I help you?
S2:	Yes. I'll take this ____ or I'll take these ____.
S1:	Will that be all?
S2:	Yes, that's all.

Any Questions?

Take out a piece of paper. Do not write your name on it. On one side of the paper, write what you think is the most interesting information that you have learned in this lesson. On the other side of the paper, write any questions you have about what you studied or talked about in class. Your teacher will collect this paper and then answer your questions the next time you meet.

Exercises

1. Mini-Dialogues

Match the lines in A with the lines in B. You will then make mini-dialogues.

To check this exercise, say each mini-dialogue with a partner. One student will read a line from A, and another student will answer with a line from B.

A

____1. Can I help you?
____2. What do you think of this suit?
____3. Excuse me. Where can I try this on?
____4. Are those new jeans?
____5. These are great sunglasses.
____6. That's a great watch.
____7. Can you come tonight?
____8. Hi. Are you busy?

B

a. Yeah, but how much is it?
b. Yeah, but how much are they?
c. It's nice. But is it very expensive?
d. Over there in the fitting rooms.
e. Uh-huh. How do they look?
f. I'm not sure. Can I let you know later?
g. Thanks. I'm just looking.
h. No. Come on in!

2. Scene Two — Listening

The following is a conversation between Lynn and Jim. They finished shopping for jeans, and now they are shopping for a wedding gown for Lynn. (A wedding gown is a special dress for a woman who is getting married.)

As you listen to the tape, fill in the blanks with the expressions that you hear. Be sure to use a capital letter at the beginning of a sentence. When you finish, perform the dialogue with two other students.

SALESCLERK:	Hello. How are you two today?
LYNN:	Fine, thanks.
SALESCLERK:	Can I help you find a wedding gown?
LYNN:	Thanks, but (1) _____ right now.
SALESCLERK:	No problem. (2) _____ if I can help.
JIM:	Thanks. Lynn. . . look at this one. (3) _____ this?
LYNN:	It's beautiful. (4) _____?
JIM:	It's too expensive.
LYNN:	Come on. . . Tell me how much. . .
JIM:	Two hundred.
LYNN:	(to the sales clerk) Excuse me. Can I (5) _____?
SALESCLERK:	Sure. The fitting rooms are right (6) _____. Just (7) _____
LYNN:	Thanks. . . . Jim . . . I'm ready . . . (8) _____?
JIM:	Wow! You look fantastic!
SALESCLERK:	Yes, it looks beautiful on you.
LYNN:	(9) _____. But Jim, please don't wear your new jeans to our wedding!

3. Dictation

Your teacher or one of your classmates will read the dictation for this lesson from Appendix C, or you will listen to the dictation on the tape. You will hear the dictation three times. First, just listen. Second, as you listen, write the dictation on a separate sheet of paper. Third, as you listen, check what you have written.

Proofread

● Did you indent the first line of each paragraph?

● Does every sentence start with a capital letter?

● Do the names have capital letters?

● Do the sentences end with a period or question mark?

Check yourself

After you check your dictation, look at your mistakes. What do you have to be more careful about next time?

___spelling	___vocabulary
___plurals	___verb tenses
___subject-verb agreement	___punctuation

Other: _____

period .
comma ,
apostrophe '
open quote "
closed quote "
question mark ?

4. Pronunciation — Thought Groups & Rhythm

Look at A and B below. Which shows the best way to say the lines from the dialogue?   ___A   or   ___B

A.

Salesclerk: (Can I help you?)

Lynn: (Thanks,) (we're just looking.)

Salesclerk: (Well,) (let me know) (if there's anything) (I can do for you.)

B.

Salesclerk: (Can) (I) (help) (you?)

Lynn: (Thanks,) (we're) (just) (looking.)

Salesclerk: (Well,) (let) (me) (know) (if) (there's) (anything) (I) (can) (do) (for) (you.)

The answer is that *A* is better. People say words in "thought groups" when they speak English. The music (rhythm) of English is not natural if you say each word alone.

Words Often in a Thought Group	Example
● a short sentence	(Can I help you?)
● a natural group of words like an expression	(let me know), (we're just looking)
● words that go alone	(thanks), (well)

PRONUNCIATION & LISTENING PRACTICE

● Say the lines of the introductory dialogue in thought groups. The words with the most stress and highest intonation are in capital letters.

Can I HELP you?
——

Thanks,
we're just LOOKing.
——

Well,
let me KNOW
if there's ANYthing
I can DO for you.
——

What do you THINK of
these JEANS?
——

They're really NICE.
How much ARE they?
——

Hmm. . .
there's no PRICE tag.
Where's the SALESperson?
I'm going to ASK her. . .
Oh,
THERE she is.
ExCUSE me,
HOW much are
these JEANS?
——

I'll be WITH you
in a MINute.
OK.
Let's SEE.
They WERE 29 dollars,
but I think toDAY
they're 30 percent OFF.
YES,
that's RIGHT.
They're about 20 DOLlars.
That's a good PRICE
for such nice JEANS.
——

Can I try them ON?
——

SURE.
The FITting rooms
are right over THERE.
Just go on IN.
Thanks a LOT.
——

LYNN,
how do they LOOK?
——

Oh, JIM!
They're too BIG.
I'll get you a SMALLer size. . .
WAIT a minute. . .
HERE,
try THESE.
——

THANKS. . .
YEAH,
I think these are BETter.
How do they LOOK?
——

FINE.
OH,
they look very NICE on you.
——

GREAT.
I'll TAKE them.

- Listen again to the tape of the dialogue. Repeat after the speakers.

- Perform the introductory dialogue in groups of three.

- Look at the dialogue in Exercise 2. Put parentheses around thought groups. Just think about what words go together naturally. Practice saying this dialogue in groups of three.

5. Walk & Talk

Set up a department store in your classroom. Bring in things to sell. Set up the following departments:

Departments	What Can You Bring to Class?
• men's department	_____
• women's department	_____
• shoes	_____
• jewelry	_____
• wallets, purses	_____
• other: _____	_____

Choose students to be salesclerks in the different departments. These students should:

- make signs that say "____ Department,"

- arrange the items they are selling, and

- decide on the prices and make price tags to put on each item.

(Remember, prices in a department store can't be changed.)

The other students are the shoppers. Each student will shop with a partner.

Everyone should try to use some of the expressions from this lesson. To help you remember them, you can write the list from exercise 10 on the board.

6. Write

Write five sentences about what you did in the Walk & Talk activity. For example, if you were a salesperson, you can write, *I sold jeans to three people.* If you were a shopper, you can write, *I tried jeans on.*

- _____

- _____

- _____

- _____

- _____

7. Info Gap

Imagine that two people are talking at a flea market. At a flea market, people can talk about changing the prices. This is called bargaining. You cannot do this in a department store.

One person (Speaker 1) is selling many different things, and the other person (Speaker 2) is a shopper.

Work with a partner. One of you will be Speaker 1 and the other will be Speaker 2. Speaker 1 will look at page 195 and Speaker 2 will look at page 196. You will have different information to give each other. Read the directions on these pages carefully.

Variation: All students who are Speaker 1 can set up tables or desks around the classroom. All students who are Speaker 2 can walk around the room and go shopping.

When you finish:

1) The shoppers will tell the class what they bought.
Examples of what they can say:
- I bought ___ because ___.
- The seller wanted $20, but I paid $__.

2) The sellers will tell the class what they sold.
Examples of what they can say:
- I sold ___.
- The customer wanted to pay only $10, but we bargained, and I got $12.

8. Tic-Tac-Toe — Play & Write

In tic-tac-toe, to get an *X* or an *O* in a space, you need to make a sentence that is correct in grammar and meaning. Here is a game with expressions from Lesson 7. (See page 15 for more detailed directions.)

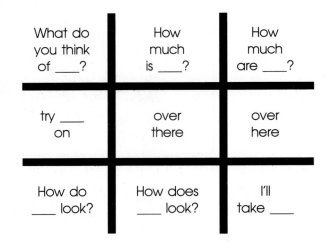

What do you think of ___?	How much is ___?	How much are ___?
try ___ on	over there	over here
How do ___ look?	How does ___ look?	I'll take ___

After you play tic-tac-toe, write sentences using all of the expressions. When you write, start every sentence with a capital letter, think about spelling, and be careful with verb tenses and other grammar that you are studying.

9. Expression Clusters & Charts

1. Add expressions from this lesson to the expression clusters in Appendix D.
2. When you hear or read expressions that you have studied in class, add them to Appendix E.
3. Write down new expressions from outside of class in Appendix F.

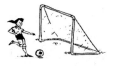

10. Goal Post

Can you now use the new expressions when you listen and speak? Put *(a)* or *(b)* next to each expression in the chart below:

	For Listening	For Speaking
	(a) I know what this expression means.	(a) I am comfortable saying this when I speak.
	(b) I'm not sure what this expression means.	(b) I am not comfortable saying this when I speak.
I'm (We're) just looking.	_____	_____
Let me know.	_____	_____
What do you think of __?	_____	_____
How much are they?	_____	_____
How much is this?	_____	_____
try __ on	_____	_____
over there	_____	_____
over here	_____	_____
go on in	_____	_____
come on in	_____	_____
How do they look?	_____	_____
How does it look?	_____	_____
I'll (We'll) take	_____	_____

If you gave any expression a *(b),* be sure to ask your teacher or a classmate for help.

Before you start the next lesson, answer these questions about this lesson:

● What did you do to learn new expressions?

● What activities helped you the most?

Lesson **8** On the Phone in Traffic

Discussing Male and Female Roles

Warm-Up

Interview a classmate and ask these questions:

1. What kind of phone or phones do you have?

■ Understanding the New Expressions

Learn with Others and/or On Your Own

WITH OTHERS

Work with a partner or in a small group.

ON YOUR OWN

Work on this section carefully, and then for each expression put an X in the *Yes* or *No* box in the margin to show if you understand the information.

(For more detailed directions, see page 3.)

All Clear?

YES	NO

1. nó próblem

> **Note:** You say this when someone asks you to do something, and you are happy to do it. It means "yes," but it is more friendly.

S1: Can you help me carry these bags?
S2: Sure. **No problem.**

S1: Is it OK if we go to the movies on Sunday? I'm busy on Saturday.
S2: **No problem.**

> **Your Turn:** Complete this dialogue.
> S1: _____?
> S2: No problem.

YES	NO

2. gét sléepy = become tired and then feel like you can sleep. Your eyes are heavy and you yawn. (past = got)

● When students **get sleepy** and they need to study, they often drink coffee.

- After driving for five hours, the driver **got sleepy**, so he stopped at a hotel.

    S1: How was the movie?
    S2: Not very interesting. It was really very boring. I **got sleepy** and wanted to go home.

> **Note:** When you are "sleepy," you are not "sleeping." You are sleepy first, and then you sleep.

Words	Part of Speech	Meaning
She is *sleepy.*	adjective	She is tired and she needs to sleep.
She is *sleeping.*	verb	She is sleeping. She is not awake. She is asleep.
She is *asleep.*	adjective	She is sleeping.
She is *awake.*	adjective	She is not sleeping.

Your Turn: (Answer in full sentences.)

- What do you do when you get sleepy when you are driving?

  _____.

- What do you do when you get sleepy when you are in class?

  _____.

- What do you do when you get sleepy when you are studying for a test?

  _____.

YES	NO

3. táke a náp = sleep for a short time, usually in the daytime
   (past = took; plural = take naps)

    S1: I'm tired. I think I'm going to **take a nap.**
    S2: Sweet dreams!

All Clear?

S1: Shh! The baby **is taking a nap.**

S2: Sorry. I didn't know.

S1: You look great!

S2: Thanks. I **took a** two-hour **nap** this afternoon, and now I have a lot of energy.

> **Your Turn:** With a partner or a group, answer this question:
>
> Do you like to take naps?
>
> ___Yes   If yes, ● when do you take naps?
>
>   ● how do you feel after you take a nap?
>
> ___No   If no, why don't you like to take naps?

4. be lúcky = have luck, be fortunate

S1: My school has a five-week vacation!

S2: **You're lucky.** I have only a two-week vacation.

S1: They went to a casino and they won a thousand dollars.

S2: They**'re** very **lucky.**

S1: When she arrived at the airport, she was late. But that was OK. The plane was late, too, so she didn't miss the plane.

S2: She **was lucky.**

● He is lucky to have   a nice family.

                         good health.

                         a nice life.

                         good friends.

                         a good education.

Your Turn: What are some things you are lucky to have?

I am lucky to have _____.

_____.

_____.

5. dó the láundry = wash the clothes (past = did)

● I'm really busy now. **I'm doing the laundry** and cleaning the house.
(Notice the present continuous tense for "right now.")

● I was busy yesterday. I **did the laundry** and cleaned the house.
(Notice the simple past tense for "yesterday.")

I	do my laundry
You	do your laundry
He	does his laundry
She	does her laundry
We	do our laundry
They	do their laundry

} every Saturday. (Notice the simple present tense for "every" Saturday.)

● I did your laundry last week. **Will** you **do my laundry** this week? (Notice the future tense for "this week.")

Your Turn: Questions for discussion:

Who does the laundry in your family?

In your opinion, is it OK for men to do the laundry?

If you do your laundry, where do you do it? ____at home?
____at a laundromat?

Do you like to do your laundry? ____yes ____no

Why or why not?

6. dó the díshes = wash the dishes

All Clear?

S1: I cooked dinner, so you need to **do the dishes**.
S2: OK. I'll do them later.

S1: I **did the dishes** last night, so you need to do them tonight.
S2: But I'm so tired.
S1: That's OK. It will only take you about ten minutes.

(a) **Your Turn:** Questions for discussion:

Who does the dishes in your family?

In your opinion, is it OK for men to do the dishes?

Do you have a dishwasher?   ___yes ___no

If yes, who "loads" (puts dirty dishes in) and "unloads" (takes clean dishes out of) the dishwasher?

(b) **Your Turn: Listening Challenge**

Listen to the tape and then answer these questions:
Who is going to do the dishes? _____
Who is going to do the laundry? _____

YES	NO

7. gét hóme = arrive at home   (past = got)

Grammar Note: This expression is used to talk about *the time* a person arrives at home. If you give the exact time, say, for example, "**at** 2:15." If you don't give the exact time, it is common to say **"around"** or "**about**." For example, you can say, "I got home **around** 2."

S1: What time do you usually **get home** from work every day?
S2: Oh, usually about 5:30. But if there's a lot of traffic, I **get home** around 6.

S1: You look tired. What time did you **get home** last night?
S2: Around 2. I didn't sleep very much.

S1: I **got home** from the city at 6 yesterday, and then I went to the movies at 7.

S2: Did you have a good time?

> **Your Turn**
>
> Ask three students the following question: *What time do you usually get home every day?* Then write sentences about each student. Use the sudents' names.
>
> 1) _____ usually gets home _____ .
>
> 2) _____ .
>
> 3) _____ .

8. cán't wáit (for/to) = want something good to happen soon

● Their son's birthday party is tomorrow, and he **can't wait.**

● Tomorrow is payday (the day we get paid at work), and she **can't wait.**

● Vacation is in two weeks. I **can't wait.**

● They are getting married next month, and they **can't wait.**

Can't Wait FOR something	**Can't Wait TO DO something**
He can't wait *for* his birthday party.	He can't wait *to have* his birthday party.
She can't wait *for* payday.	She can't wait *to get* her paycheck.
I can't wait *for* my vacation.	I can't wait *to have* my vacation.
They can't wait *for* the wedding.	They can't wait *to get* married.

> **Your Turn**
>
> On the left, write three things that you can't wait for, and on the right, write three things that you can't wait to do:
>
> | **I can't wait for** | **I can't wait to** |
> | --- | --- |
> | _____ | _____ |
> | _____ | _____ |
> | _____ | _____ |

9. (I) hópe só. = I want that to happen.

S1: Are you going to learn English quickly?

S2: **I hope so.**

S1: Are you going to be there on Saturday?

S2: **We hope so**. We have to go somewhere first, but we'll try.

Opposite: · (I) **hópe nót**. = I don't want that to happen.

S1: Is it going to rain?

S2: **I hope not!** We want to go to the beach.

S1: Do we have a test today?

S2: **I hope not!** I didn't study.

> **Your Turn:** Finish these short dialogues:
>
> **S1:** _____?
>
> **S2:** I hope so.
>
> **S1:** _____?
>
> **S2:** I hope not.

Any Questions?

Take out a piece of paper. Do not write your name on it. On one side of the paper, write what you think is the most interesting information that you have learned in this lesson. On the other side of the paper, write any questions you have about what you studied or talked about in class. Your teacher will collect this paper and then answer your questions the next time you meet.

Exercises

1. Mini-Dialogues

Match the lines in A with the lines in B. You will then make mini-dialogues.

To check this exercise, say each mini-dialogue with a partner. One student will read a line from A, and another student will answer with a line from B.

A	**B**
____1. I'm getting really sleepy.	a. She's lucky. I have a lot.
____2. She doesn't have any homework this weekend.	b. I don't know. I hope so.
____3. Why are you so tired?	c. I know. I can't wait to go.
____4. Does he like his new job?	d. Why don't you take a nap?
____5. His party is going to be great.	e. No problem.
____6. Is she angry with you?	f. I did the laundry and the dishes, and I cleaned the house and worked in the garden.
____7. What time do you think you'll get home tonight?	g. I hope not.
____8. Can you help me with this homework? It's hard.	h. Probably around 9.

2. Scene Two — Listening

The following is a conversation between the husband and wife after the wife gets home. They are talking in their living room after dinner.

As you listen to the tape, fill in the blanks with the expressions that you hear. Be sure to use a capital letter at the beginning of a sentence. When you finish, perform the dialogue with a partner.

WIFE:	Umm. That chicken was really good. (1) _____ that I married you. You're a great cook.
HUSBAND:	Thanks.
WIFE:	And it's great that you (2) _____ and (3) _____. Did you have enough time to do your work at the computer?
HUSBAND:	Not today, but tomorrow I'll work a lot. Can you pick up the kids and make dinner tomorrow?
WIFE:	Sure. (4) _____. I'll try to (5) _____ early tomorrow. What do you want for dinner?
HUSBAND:	Hmm. . . How about your delicious spaghetti?
WIFE:	Good idea! It's pretty easy to make.
HUSBAND:	I (6) _____! I can almost taste it now.
WIFE:	You know, it's only 8:30, but (7) _____. I had a busy day.
HUSBAND:	And you didn't (8) _____ like I did. Maybe it's a good idea to go to bed early tonight.
WIFE:	Yeah, but I want to watch some TV first. What's on?

period .
comma ,

3. Dictation

Your teacher or one of your classmates will read the dictation for this lesson from Appendix C, or you will listen to the dictation on the tape. You will hear the dictation three times. First, just listen. Second, as you listen, write the dictation on a separate sheet of paper. Third, as you listen, check what you have written.

Proofread

● Did you indent the first line of each paragraph?

● Does every sentence start with a capital letter?

● Do the sentences end with a period?

Check yourself

After you check your dictation, look at your mistakes. What do you have to be more careful about next time?

___spelling   ___vocabulary

___plurals   ___verb tenses

___subject-verb agreement   ___punctuation

Other: _____

4. Pronunciation—Stress, Intonation, Rhythm Review

● Say the lines of the introductory dialogue in thought groups. The words with the most stress and highest intonation are in capital letters.

HONey?
It's ME.

——

Where ARE you?

——

In TRAFfic.
I'm GOing to be
REALly late.
Can YOU
pick UP
the KIDS?

——

No PROBlem.
What TIME
do you THINK
you'll be HOME?

——

PRObably
in about an HOUr.
The TRAFfic
is really BAD.
How was your DAY?

——

Well,
I WORKED
for a few HOUrs
at the comPUter,
and then I got SLEEPy
so I took a NAP.

——

You took a NAP!
You're LUCKy
you work at HOME.
I can't take a NAP
in the OFfice,
you KNOW.

——

But I ALso
did the LAUNdry
and the DISHes.
You CAN'T
do those THINGS
at the OFfice.

——

THAT'S true.
HEY,
what's for DINner?

——

CHICKen.
It'll be READy
when you get HOME.

——

I can't WAIT.
I LOVE
your CHICKen.

——

And I
love YOU.
SEE you
by six-THIRty?

——

I HOPE so.
SEE ya.

● Listen again to the tape of the dialogue. Repeat after the speakers.

● Perform the introductory dialogue in pairs.

5. Walk & Talk

Walk around the room and ask two different students questions 1 and 2 below. Be sure to also ask the question, "Why?"

> **1. Do you think it's OK for men to do the laundry, do the dishes, and cook?**
>
> **Why?**
>
> Student 1: _____(name) ___yes ___sometimes ___no
>
> Student 2: _____(name) ___yes ___sometimes ___no
>
> **2. Do you think it's OK for women to work if they have young children?**
>
> Student 1: ___yes ___sometimes ___no
>
> Student 2: ___yes ___sometimes ___no
>
> | **Class Results** | yes | sometimes | no |
> |---|---|---|---|
> | Question 1 | ___ | ___ | ___ |
> | Question 2 | ___ | ___ | ___ |

When you finish, put the class results on the board and have the students give reasons why they said *yes, sometimes,* or *no.*

6. Write

Write two sentences about what each student said to you in Exercise 5. Use the students' names.

Question 1

1. _____said it's OK for men to do the laundry because. . . _____

2. _____

Question 2

1. _____

2. _____

7. Contact Assignment/Survey

With a partner, ask three native speakers of English the following questions. You can ask people in your school, at a library or store, or in your neighborhood. You do not need to walk up to strangers on the street.

Introduce yourself like this. You can practice saying this in class:

Hi. We're from _____ and ____ and we're studying English. We have a homework assignment to ask eight short questions about male and female roles and household chores. Do you have a minute to answer our questions?

Be sure to look directly at the people you are talking to. You can take short notes, but don't just look at your book. Also, don't let the people read the questions. You need to ask the questions so that you can practice speaking English with native speakers.

1. Do you think it's OK for men to do the laundry, do the dishes, and cook?

                                                                    REASONS

Person 1: ___yes ___sometimes ___no _____

Person 2: ___yes ___sometimes ___no _____

Person 3: ___yes ___sometimes ___no _____

2. Do you think it's OK for women to work if they have children?

Person 1: ___yes ___sometimes ___no _____

Person 2: ___yes ___sometimes ___no _____

Person 3: ___yes ___sometimes ___no _____

3. _____?
(You and your partner write a question to ask.)

Person 1: ___yes ___sometimes ___no _____

Person 2: ___yes ___sometimes ___no _____

Person 3: ___yes ___sometimes ___no _____

After you get the information from the three people, answer these questions:

1. When you said you were studying English and you asked people to talk to you, what did they say? _____

_____

2. Did the native speakers understand your questions?

___always ___usually ___sometimes ___rarely

3. How much did you understand when the native speakers answered your questions? _____%

4. How did you feel when you talked to the three native speakers?

_____

_____

8. Tic-Tac-Toe — Play & Write

In tic-tac-toe, to get an *X* or an *O* in a space, you need to make a sentence that is correct in grammar and meaning. Here is a game with expressions from Lesson 8. (See page 15 for more detailed directions.)

get sleepy	take a nap	be lucky
do the laundry	get home	can't wait to
can't wait for	S1:_____? S2: No problem.	S1:_____? S2: I hope so!

After you play tic-tac-toe, write sentences using all of the expressions. When you write, start every sentence with a capital letter, think about spelling, and be careful with verb tenses and other grammar that you are studying.

9. Expression Clusters & Charts

1. Add expressions from this lesson to the expression clusters in Appendix D.
2. When you hear or read expressions that you have studied in class, add them to Appendix E.
3. Write down new expressions from outside of class in Appendix F.

10. Goal Post

Can you now use the new expressions when you listen and speak? Put *(a)* or *(b)* next to each expression in the chart below:

	For Listening (a) I know what this expression means. (b) I'm not sure what this expression means.	**For Speaking** (a) I am comfortable saying this when I speak. (b) I am not comfortable saying this when I speak.
get sleepy	_____	_____
no problem	_____	_____
take a nap	_____	_____
be lucky	_____	_____
do the laundry	_____	_____
do the dishes	_____	_____
get home	_____	_____
can't wait	_____	_____
I hope so	_____	_____
I hope not	_____	_____

If you gave any expression a *(b)*, be sure to ask your teacher or a classmate for help.

● Now that you have finished ***All Clear Intro,*** what helped you the most in learning new expressions in English?

● What will you do to continue learning new expressions?

Crossword Puzzle for Lessons 7 and 8

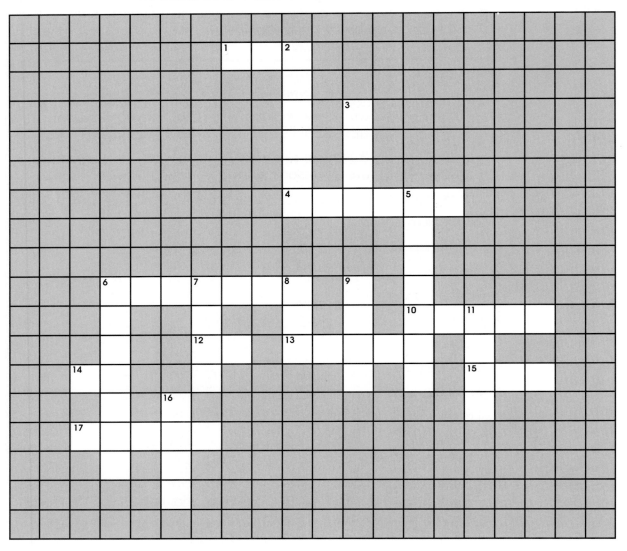

Across

1. Don't worry. Sit down. I already ____ the dishes.
4. I'm going to bed. I'm getting ____.
6. Thanks. We're just ____.
10. You're ____ that you know more than one language.
12. What did you think ____ the movie?
13. They're sitting over ____.
14. Go ____ in. I'll be right there.
15. Ssh! The baby is taking a ____.
17. I ____ it on and it didn't fit, so I didn't buy it.

Down

2. Sometimes I do the ____ and sometimes he does them.
3. I ____ so.
5. Sure I can help you. No ____.
6. Who does the ____ in your house?
7. Let me ____ if you need any help.
8. What time do you think you're going to ____ home?
9. These jeans are great. I'll take ____.
11. I ____ wait to see you!
16. Come over ____. I want to tell you something.

Classroom Language

These are questions and directions that students and teachers often use. Add to these lists as you, your classmates, and teacher talk in class.

Questions That Students Often Ask in Class:

1. How do you spell ___?

2. How do you pronounce ___?

3. What does ___ mean?

4. What is the meaning of ___?

5. What is the definition of ___?

6. _____

7. _____

8. _____

Requests That Students Often Make in Class:

1. Could you please write that on the board?

2. Could you please repeat that?

3. Could you please say that again?

4. Could you please say that more slowly?

5. _____

6. _____

7. _____

Questions That Teachers Often Ask to See if Students Understand:

1. Do you understand?

2. Are you following me?

3. Got it?

4. _____

5. _____

6. _____

Directions That Teachers Often Give Students:

1. Pass your papers up.

2. Pass these papers back.

3. Hand in (turn in) your homework.

4. Get into groups.

5. Work with a partner.

6. Check your homework.

7. Take turns.

8. _____

9. _____

10. _____

Listening Challenge Tapescript

Lesson 1

A: Hi. Where are you from?
B: Japan. How about you?
A: I'm from Mexico.
B: When did you come to the US?
A: Oh, about a month ago. And you?
B: About six months ago.
A: Do you like it here?
B: Now I do. But I didn't like it at the beginning.
A: Why not?
B: Hmm. . . well, I didn't understand anything. Everyone was speaking very fast.
A: I know what you mean. Uh. . . You know, I don't know your name. . .
B: It's Rika. What's your name?
A: Jose. It's nice to meet you.
B: Nice to meet you, too.

Lesson 2

1. It's a nice day.
2. We have a test tomorrow.
3. I want to learn how to play the guitar.
4. I'm tired.
5. They're bored.
6. We're hungry.

Lesson 3

A: Ruby's Place. May I help you?
B: Yes. I'd like to make a reservation for two for Saturday night.
A: What time?
B: Eight o'clock?
A: OK. And your name please?
B: Healy. H - E - A - L - Y.
A: OK. That will be Saturday night at 8 for two.
B: Right. And can I reserve a table by the window? It's our wedding anniversary and . . .
A: No problem.
B: Thanks a lot. See you on Saturday.
A: Thank you.

Lesson 4

1. Wake up! You're late!
2. Don't fall asleep again! Get up!
3. Don't go back to sleep! Get out of bed!
4. Get dressed! You're late!
5. Put on a jacket! It's cold!
6. Have a nice day!

Lesson 5

1. Where do you want to have lunch?
2. When do you want to study for the test?
3. Do you want me to bring dessert or salad to your party?
4. When do you want to go to the city?
5. Where do you want to sit?

Lesson 6

1. My head hurts.
2. My stomach hurts.
3. My tooth hurts.
4. My back hurts.
5. My ear hurts.

Lesson 7

1. This is a nice dress.
2. Those look like warm gloves.
3. This shirt is too small.
4. I like your hat.
5. Are the shorts OK?

Lesson 8

MAN: Why don't YOU do the dishes, and I'LL do the laundry?

WOMAN: I did the dishes yesterday.

MAN: OK, I'LL do the dishes, and YOU do the laundry.

WOMAN: Why? I always do the laundry.

MAN: That's not true. I do the laundry, too.

WOMAN: Hmm. Why don't we just go to the movies? We can clean tomorrow.

MAN: Great idea!

Dictations for Exercise 3

Lesson 1

Eric is a student. He is very nervous on the first day of class. He is afraid of talking in front of people. His friend Andy tells him, "Don't worry." She says he will get to know people in the class and make friends.

After class Eric feels better, but Andy is nervous. She is afraid of having a lot of homework. Eric tells Andy that he will help her.

Lesson 2

When Alex calls his friend Sara, her sister Anna answers the phone. Anna asks, "Who's this?" and Alex says, "It's Alex." Anna tells her sister, "It's for you!" and Sara comes to the phone.

Alex invites Sara to go to the movies on Friday night. Sara can't make it on Friday, but Saturday is good. But they don't go to the movies. They go to dinner and it's great. They want to go to the same restaurant again, but Sara wants to drive there. She also wants to pay.

Lesson 3

Alice and Peter go away for the weekend. They go to the beach. It is winter, so they can't go swimming. But they take walks on the beach and they get plenty of fresh air. On Friday night they go dancing, and on Sunday they go ice skating. They have a good time and are very happy.

Lesson 4

Tom has to wake up early to go to the airport. But when his roommate wakes him up, he doesn't want to get up. The room is very cold and dark, and he wants to go back to sleep.

Tom gets up, but he doesn't have time to take a shower. He gets dressed quickly and goes to the airport. He's lucky because he doesn't miss his plane.

Lesson 5

WAITRESS: Are you ready to order?

CUSTOMER: Yes. What kind of soup do you have?

WAITRESS: Today we have really good chicken soup.

CUSTOMER: That sounds good. I'd like a cup of soup and a turkey sandwich.

WAITRESS: Would you like anything to drink?

CUSTOMER: Yes, I think I'll have some hot tea.

WAITRESS: Will that be all?

CUSTOMER: Yes, for now. Thanks.

Lesson 6

Mike is standing at the top of the stairs. He is reading something. Then he falls down the stairs. His leg hurts a lot. He tells his wife, Judy, that his leg is killing him.

Judy gets ice for him and then she takes him to the hospital. The doctor says that Mike's leg is broken. Mike isn't happy because he has to stay put. He can't go to work for a few days.

Lesson 7

Lynn and Jim go shopping together for jeans. Jim asks Lynn, "What do you think of these jeans?" She likes them, but she asks, "How much are they?" They are about $20 and Jim tries them on. When Lynn sees Jim, she laughs because the jeans are very, very big. She gets a different size for Jim and these jeans look very nice on him. Jim tells the salesclerk, "I'll take them."

Then they go shopping for a wedding gown for Lynn. They are going to get married very soon.

Lesson 8

A wife is coming home late from work because of traffic. She has a cell phone, so she calls her husband to tell him she is late. He will pick up the kids and have a chicken dinner ready when she gets home.

The wife thinks her husband is lucky because he works at home and he can take naps when he is sleepy. He says that he does the laundry and the dishes because he is home. They have an interesting life.

Expression Clusters

Every time you finish a lesson, you can add expressions to the "clusters" below. There are extra lines, so you can also add other expressions that you talk about in class. Over time, you will see how many expressions with the same words you have learned.

Review Game: Using a dark marking pen, write the following words on sheets of paper (one word on each sheet). (Word List: *make, do, take, have, get, go, up, out, down, in, to, of, at*) Students should stand in front of the classroom, each holding a sheet of paper so that everyone can see.

The other students should have 3" x 5" cards with expressions minus the words in the above list. Each student should walk up to and stand by the student who is holding the word that will complete the expression. After everyone is standing in the right place, the groups of students clustered around each word can go to the board and make sentences with the expressions that they form.

Expressions with Verbs:

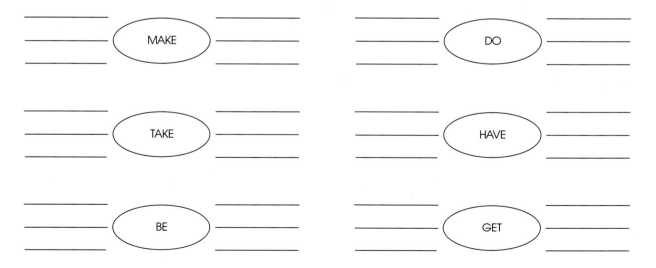

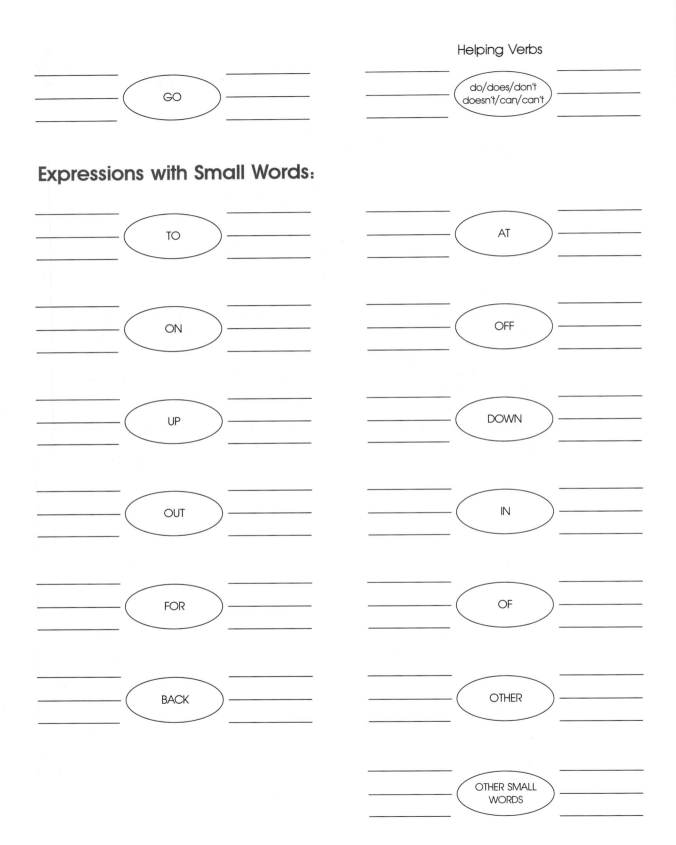

Helping Verbs

GO

do/does/don't
doesn't/can/can't

Expressions with Small Words:

TO

AT

ON

OFF

UP

DOWN

OUT

IN

FOR

OF

BACK

OTHER

OTHER SMALL
WORDS

Expression Chart 1

Expressions from *All Clear! Intro*
That Students Hear or Read Outside of Class

Outside of class, you will hear and read many of the expressions that you are studying because the expressions are so common.

When you hear or read any of these expressions, write them down in this chart. This will help make you a more careful listener and reader, and you will find that you remember the expressions better.

It would be a good idea if perhaps once a week students in your class shared their lists.

Expression	Where I Heard or Read It	Who Was Speaking

Expression Chart 2

New Expressions That Students Bring to Class from the Outside World

Outside of class, you will hear and read many expressions in English. You will find them on TV and on the radio, in the movies, on T-shirts, on bumper stickers, and in advertisements. They are everywhere.

Start a collection of these expressions by writing them down on 3x5 cards. You can find out what the expressions mean either by asking someone outside of class or by asking your teacher.

It would be a good idea if perhaps once a week students in your class shared their lists.

Sample card:

Expression:

Where I heard or read it:

Who was speaking:

Meaning:

Sample Sentence:

_____

_____

_____

Study Tips

1. Study Cards

Buy a set of 3″ x 5″ cards. On each card, write the following with the expressions that you find most difficult to remember from each lesson.

Expression:

Sentence:

Grammar Reminder:

Pronunciation Reminder:

Here is an example:

Expression:	*get out of bed*
Sentence:	*It is hard for me to get out of bed early in the morning.*
Grammar Reminder:	*remember "of"*
Pronunciation Reminder:	*Some people say "owda" for "out of."*

2. Cover Your Walls

Do you ever wash dishes? Why don't you hang a card with expressions that you need to study near your sink? You can review while you wash dishes.

Of course, you can hang up cards all over your home. Soon you will be dreaming about expressions in English.

3. Other Ideas

(a) Write new expressions from in or out of class in a small book that fits in a pocket or purse. Study these expressions while you wait for a bus, wait to see a doctor, etc.

(b) Study with others. What are some of the ways you can study together?

_____

_____

_____

(c) Your Suggestions?

_____

_____

_____

Student Self-Evaluation Questionnaire

Name: _____

Date: _____

Circle the number that shows how much you agree or disagree with the sentences on the left.

	No		**Yes**
1. I know many more expressions in English.	1	2	3
2. Sometimes I try to use some of these expressions when I speak.	1	2	3
3. When I listen to native speakers of English, I sometimes hear expressions that I studied.	1	2	3
4. When I see or hear expressions that I don't know, I write them down and ask what they mean.	1	2	3
5. I know more about pronunciation in English.	1	2	3
6. I try to think about pronunciation when I talk.	1	2	3
7. I listen carefully to how native speakers of English pronounce words.	1	2	3
8. I'm working hard both in and out of class.	1	2	3
9. I like to work with other students in class.	1	2	3
10. I like to study with other students outside of class.	1	2	3

Questions/Comments?

Student Self-Evaluation— The Train

Where are you in our class?

What number or numbers apply to you?

Why? Please write your reasons on the back of this page.

Holidays & Special Days in the United States

Following is a list of the most common holidays and special days in the United States. Here you will find information about these days and also what people say to each other.

New Year's

New Year's Eve Celebrated: December 31
New Year's Day Celebrated: January 1
What people say: *Happy New Year!*

People often welcome the new year by having New Year's Eve parties. At midnight, people kiss each other, make noise with noisemakers and drink champagne. The traditional music that is played at midnight is called "Auld Lang Syne" which is a Scottish song. The words of the song ask, "Should we forget old times?"

On New Year's Day, many people make "New Year's resolutions." These are promises that they will make good changes in their lives. For example, some people say that they will get more exercise and lose weight. Some people say that they will read more books. It is easy to make these promises on January 1 and then forget them on January 2. Also on New Year's Day, some people watch football games on TV.

Martin Luther King's Birthday

Birthday: January 15
Celebrated: the third Monday of January

Martin Luther King was an African-American leader in the 1950s and 1960s. He worked for African-American people to have equal rights (civil rights) in the United States. He believed that people should fight for their rights without being violent. In 1964, he won the Nobel Peace Prize. In 1968, when he was 39 years old, he was killed. On his birthday, people in the United States remember and honor him.

(Saint) Valentine's Day

Celebrated: February 14
What people say: *Happy Valentine's Day!*

Valentine's Day probably comes from an ancient (old) Roman festival. At this festival, young men and women got each other's names from a box, and then gave each other gifts. Often they saw each other after the festival and sometimes they got married.

Today boys and girls and men and women give each other cards, flowers, and candy on Valentine's Day to show that they like or love each other. In schools, children decorate their classrooms with red hearts and make "valentines," special cards with red hearts, to give to each other and their families.

Presidents Day

Celebrated: the third Monday of February

On Presidents Day, Americans honor their first president, George Washington, whose birthday was February 22, and Abraham Lincoln, whose birthday was February 12.

Passover (Jewish Holiday)

Celebrated: in March or April
What people say to Jewish people: *Happy Passover!*

During Passover, Jewish people around the world celebrate the escape of Jews from slavery in Egypt. This holiday lasts for eight days. On the first two evenings, people have a special meal called a *seder*. At the seder, they read about the "exodus" (leaving) from Egypt and eat special food, such as "matzoh," a kind of cracker.

Easter (Christian Holiday)

Celebrated: in March or April
What people say to Christian people: *Happy Easter!*

At Easter, Christians celebrate the resurrection (rebirth) of Jesus Christ. After they go to church, many people have a special lunch or dinner. In New York, many people walk in the Easter Parade, which is shown on TV.

A few days before Easter, children dye eggs many colors, and put these eggs into Easter baskets. Children also go on "Easter egg hunts." This means that they go to a house or park and look for eggs that are hidden. When they wake up on Easter morning, many children find Easter baskets with chocolate eggs, jelly beans, small toys, and Easter eggs from the Easter Bunny (rabbit).

April Fools' Day

Celebrated: April 1
What people say if they play a joke on someone: *April Fools!*

April 1st is the day when people play jokes on each other. This means that they say things that aren't true, and then they say, "April Fools!" For example, a person might say to a friend, "I'm getting married." The friend will get excited and say, "Congratulations!" and ask a lot of questions. Then the first person will say, "April Fools! — I'm not getting married. I was joking," and his or her friend will remember that it's April 1.

April Fools' Day probably started in France in 1564 when the King changed New Year's Day from April 1 to January 1. People laughed at people who continued to celebrate New Year's on April 1.

Mother's Day

Celebrated: the second Sunday of May
What people say: *Happy Mother's Day!*

Mother's Day is a day to honor and give special attention to mothers. Children give their mothers cards and flowers or presents, and some children (often with the help of their fathers) give their mothers "breakfast in bed." That evening, families often go out to dinner. Children who do not live at home call or visit their mothers. This special day started in 1914.

Memorial Day

Celebrated: the last Monday of May

Memorial Day is really May 31, but it is celebrated on a Monday so that people can have a three-day weekend. On this day, people remember and honor soldiers who died in all wars. This holiday started in the American South after the Civil War when graves of soldiers from both the north and south were decorated.

Memorial Day is now a symbol of the start of summer. Many people have barbecues on this day and enjoy the warm weather.

Father's Day

Celebrated: the third Sunday of June
What people say: *Happy Father's Day!*

Father's Day is a day to honor and give special attention to fathers. Children give their fathers cards and flowers or presents. That evening, families often go out to dinner. Children who do not live at home call or visit their fathers. This special day started in 1910.

4th of July

Celebrated: July 4
What people say: *Happy 4th of July!*

This holiday has three names: July 4th, the Fourth of July, or Independence Day. It is the birthday of the United States. It celebrates the Declaration of Independence on July 4th, 1776, in Philadelphia. In the Declaration of Independence, the 13 colonies (there were not yet 50 states) announced that they were independent from the "mother country," Britain. Following this declaration, the colonies and Britain fought against each other in the Revolutionary War. The colonies won and became the United States.

On this summer holiday, many communities have parades. Also, many people go swimming and have barbecues, and then after the sun sets in the evening they watch fireworks.

Labor Day

Celebrated: the first Monday of September

Labor Day, which began in 1894 in the U.S. and Canada, honors workers. Many other countries honor their workers on May 1.

Labor Day is now a symbol of the end of summer and the beginning of the school year. Many people have barbecues on this day and enjoy the warm weather.

Halloween

Celebrated: October 31
What people say: *Happy Halloween!*

Halloween was a Celtic festival (Celts were the people of Great Britain and Ireland) a long time ago. This festival marked the end of the summer and honored the Lord of the Dead. On this day, the souls of the dead were supposed to visit their homes. October 31 was also the beginning of the new year.

Later, when the Romans conquered Britain, they also celebrated the beginning of winter. At their festivals, they brought apples to honor the Roman goddess of fruit and trees. And hundreds of years later, when the area became Christian, the people celebrated a religious holiday, All Saints Day, on November 1. They called the night before All Saints Day "all Hallows' Eve" which later got the name "Halloween." Irish and Scottish immigrants brought customs related to this holiday to the United States, and these customs became popular at the end of the nineteenth century.

Halloween is now mostly a special day for children. They dress up in costumes and have parades and parties at school. They "bob for apples," which means they put their hands behind their backs and try to catch apples in their teeth while the apples are floating around in a big container of water.

At night children in costumes often go to parties or go "trick-or-treating" in their neighborhoods. When they do this, they knock on people's doors and say, "Trick-or-treat!" and their neighbors give them Halloween candy.

Children also carve (cut) pumpkins and make jack-o'-lanterns. These are empty pumpkins with eyes, noses, and mouths cut out of them. At night, people put candles or lights in their jack-o'-lanterns and then put them outside or in windows. Some people also play scary sounds so that their houses seem "haunted" (with ghosts).

Veterans Day

Celebrated: November 11

On Veterans Day, American soldiers from the past and present are honored. This holiday was originally known as Armistice Day, the day when World War I ended.

Thanksgiving

Celebrated: the fourth Thursday of November
What people say: *Happy Thanksgiving!*

Thanksgiving started as a three-day "Harvest Home" festival by Pilgrims in early October, 1621, in Plymouth, Massachusetts. Pilgrims were English settlers who lived in the Plymouth area and brought this festival with them from England. At a Harvest Home festival, there were athletic competitions, shooting matches, and a lot to eat and drink.

Pilgrims came across the Atlantic Ocean from England for many reasons. About one-third of them came for religious freedom.

The Pilgrims had a peace treaty with their neighbors, the Massasoit Indians (Native Americans), and they celebrated the Harvest Home holiday together. They enjoyed entertainment and ate together, but it is possible that they ate goose or deer and not turkey.

In the 1700s, Thanksgiving became a holiday for giving thanks to God for the harvest. People in different parts of the United States celebrated the holiday differently. In 1863, President Abraham Lincoln made Thanksgiving a national holiday, and in 1942 Congress in Washington made·the fourth Thursday in November Thanksgiving day.

Today families get together on Thanksgiving for a big feast (a special big meal) with turkey and special food such as cranberry sauce, sweet potatoes, and pumpkin pie. People do not give each other gifts on this day. The day after Thanksgiving is known as the biggest shopping day of the year because on that day there are big sales in stores to start the Christmas shopping season.

Christmas (Christian Holiday)

Christmas Eve: December 24
Christmas Day: December 25

What people say:
- •to Christians: *Merry Christmas!*
- •to people who aren't Christian, or if you're not sure: *Happy Holidays!*

Christmas is a celebration of the birth of Jesus Christ. People often decorate their houses with lights on the outside and have a Christmas tree inside. Many people exchange (give each other) presents, and they go to church for Christmas services. They sing special Christmas songs called *carols*.

Many children believe that Santa Claus will come down the chimney on Christmas Eve while they are sleeping and leave presents under the tree and small gifts in Christmas stockings. Little children often leave cookies and milk by the fireplace so that Santa can have a snack if he gets hungry while he is delivering presents.

Chanukah (Jewish Holiday)

Celebrated: November or December
What people say to Jewish people: *Happy Chanukah!*
Chanukah is an eight-day holiday celebrated by Jewish people to remember a time long ago when Jews fought against Greek kings who didn't let them follow their religion. When they were fighting, Jews were in a temple where they had very little oil for light, but the oil they had surprisingly lasted for eight days.

Chanukah, "The Festival of Lights," celebrates this "miracle." During Chanukah, Jewish people light candles on a menorah. With the candle in the center of the menorah, they light one candle on the first night, two candles on the second night, three candles on the third night, and so on, until the eighth night, when they light all eight candles to remember the eight days in the temple.

To celebrate this holiday, families also make latkes (potato pancakes) in oil and they give presents to the children. They sing special Chanukah songs and play a game with a toy called a dreydl.

Kwanzaa (African-American Holiday)

Celebrated: December 26 to January 1

Kwanzaa is an African-American celebration that was introduced to the United States in the early 1960s. It is not a religious holiday. It is a holiday that celebrates the seven principles of the African value system.

Every night during the holiday, African-Americans light candles for each of the seven principles. On the last night of Kwanzaa, people light all of the candles.

The last night of Kwanzaa is also the new year. Then everyone has a special meal called a feast.

During the week of Kwanzaa, children learn African history and culture, home decorating, cooking, songs, stories, dances, and games. The whole family celebrates together.

The seven principles:

Day 1: Unity—To try to keep the family, community, nation, and race together

Day 2: Self-Determination—For African-Americans to say who they are and what they believe, not for other people to say who they are

Day 3: Collective Work and Responsibility—To build a community together and to work with others and solve problems together

Day 4: Cooperative Economics—To have stores and businesses owned by African-Americans in African-American communities

Day 5: Purpose—To build and develop the African-American community

Day 6: Creativity—For African-Americans to always do as much as they can to make their community more beautiful

Day 7: Faith—For African-Americans to believe in their people, their parents, their teachers, their leaders, and the right to fight for a better life

A Holiday in Your Native Country

Celebrated:
What people say:

Explain this holiday by answering the following questions:

•What does this holiday mean? What does it celebrate?

•How do people celebrate? What do they do?

•Are there special kinds of food? Decorations?

•Are there any special activities for children?

_____

_____

_____

_____

_____

Hot Seat

Choose one student to come to the "Hot Seat" (a chair) in the front of the room. Or, get into groups and choose one student in each group to be on the "Hot Seat." This student will answer questions. If someone asks a personal question, the student on the hot seat does not have to answer.

When you ask questions, remember to think about question intonation (see Lesson 6).

Possible Questions:

- What's your name?

- Where are you from?

- Where do you live now?

- Why do you want to learn English?

- Do you like the U.S.? (Canada, Japan, etc.?) Why or why not?

- What do you do in your free time?

- Do you like to go to the movies? What kind of movies do you like?

- What is your favorite kind of music?

- What is your favorite kind of food?

- Other:

"Taboo" Questions: (Don't ask these because they are too personal.)

Are you married? How old are you? What is your religion? How much money do you make? How much rent do you pay? If someone asks you these questions and you don't want to answer, you can answer with a question. For example:

S1:   How old are you?
S2:   How old are YOU?

Or, you can just say, "That's a personal question."

Vowels & Consonants

Vowel Chart

A, E, I, O and U are vowels. They are LETTERS of the alphabet.

But in English, there are 16 vowel SOUNDS. Look at the chart below:

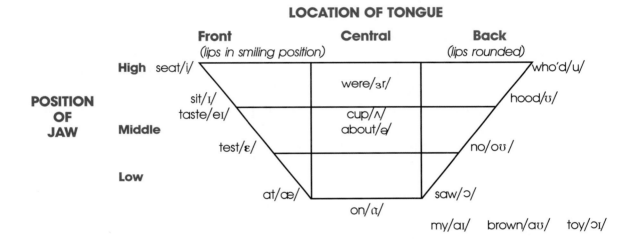

Consonant Chart

Letters	Sounds	Voiced	Voiceless	Example
b	/b/	x		**b**ut
c	/k/, /s/		x	**c**omputer, scien**c**e
d	/d/	x		**d**inosaur
f	/f/		x	**f**orget
g	/g/, /dʒ/	x		for**g**et, technolo**g**y
h	/h/		x	**h**ome
j	/dʒ/	x		**j**udge
k	/k/		x	thin**k**
l	/l/	x		mai**l**
m	/m/	x		progra**m**
n	/n/	x		wo**n**

Letters	Sounds	Voiced	Voiceless	Example
p	/p/		x	com**p**uter
q	/kw/		x	**q**uite
r	/r/	x		**r**eally
s	/s/, /z/, /ʒ/	x	x	u**s**, i**s**, u**s**ual
t	/t/		x	grea**t**
v	/v/	x		**v**ery
w	/w/	x		**w**on
x	/ks/		x	si**x**
y	/y/	x		**y**ou
z	/z/	x		**z**oo
ch	/tʃ/, /ʃ/, /k/		x	**ch**ange, ma**ch**ine, te**ch**nology
sh	/ʃ/		x	**sh**e
th	/ð/, /θ/	x	x	**th**is, **th**ink
ng	/ŋ/	x		thi**ng**

Guide to Pronunciation Symbols

VOWELS			CONSONANTS		
Symbol	Key Word	Pronunciation	Symbol	Key Word	Pronunciation
/ɑ/	**hot**	/hɑt/	/b/	**boy**	/bɔɪ/
	far	/fɑr/	/d/	**day**	/deɪ/
/æ/	**cat**	/kæt/	/dʒ/	**just**	/dʒʌst/
/aɪ/	**fine**	/faɪn/	/f/	**face**	/feɪs/
/aʊ/	**house**	/haʊs/	/g/	**get**	/gɛt/
/ɛ/	**bed**	/bɛd/	/h/	**hat**	/hæt/
/eɪ/	**name**	/neɪm/	/k/	**car**	/kɑr/
/i/	**need**	/nid/	/l/	**light**	/laɪt/
/ɪ/	**sit**	/sɪt/	/m/	**my**	/maɪ/
/oʊ/	**go**	/goʊ/	/n/	**nine**	/naɪn/
/ʊ/	**book**	/bʊk/	/ŋ/	**sing**	/sɪŋ/
/u/	**boot**	/but/	/p/	**pen**	/pɛn/
/ɔ/	**dog**	/dɔg/	/r/	**right**	/raɪt/
	four	/fɔr/	/s/	**see**	/si/
/ɔɪ/	**toy**	/tɔɪ/	/t/	**tea**	/ti/
/ʌ/	**cup**	/kʌp/	/tʃ/	**cheap**	/tʃip/
/ɜr/	**bird**	/bɜrd/	/v/	**vote**	/voʊt/
/ə/	**about**	/əˈbaʊt/	/w/	**west**	/wɛst/
	after	/ˈæftər/	/y/	**yes**	/yɛs/
			/z/	**zoo**	/zu/
			/ð/	**they**	/ðeɪ/
			/θ/	**think**	/θɪŋk/
			/ʃ/	**shoe**	/ʃu/
			/ʒ/	**vision**	/ˈviʒən/

Source: *The Newbury House Dictionary of American English*

Crossword Puzzle Solutions

Lessons 1 & 2   ## Lessons 3 & 4

Lessons 5 & 6

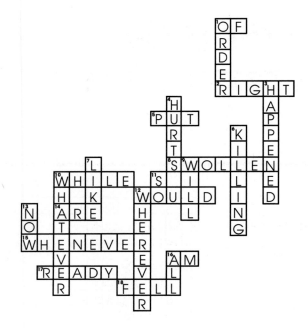

Lessons 7 & 8

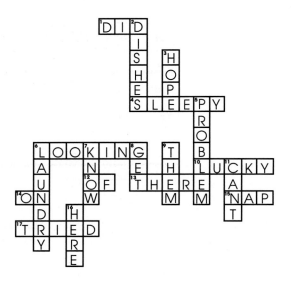

Answer Key for Listening Challenges and Exercises 1 & 2

Lesson 1

Listening Challenge

1	4
6	2
7	3
5	

Exercise 1: Mini-Dialogues

1. d	4. a
2. b	5. f
3. e	6. c

Exercise 2: Scene Two

1. What's wrong
2. I'm afraid of
3. have to
4. Don't worry
5. make friends
6. At the beginning
7. were afraid
8. get to know
9. have trouble
10. are taking
11. get better

Lesson 2

Listening Challenge

1. c	4. a
2. f	5. e
3. d	6. b

Exercise 1: Mini-Dialogues

1. e	4. b
2. a	5. c
3. f	6. d

Exercise 2: Scene Two

1. Who's this
2. This is
3. Hold on
4. It's for you
5. I'll be right there
6. Why don't
7. That sounds
8. pick you up
9. hang up

Lesson 3

Listening Challenge

1. It's his wedding anniversary and he wants to take his wife out to dinner.
2. His wife.
3. By the window.
4. Saturday night at eight o'clock.

Exercise 1: Mini-Dialogues

1. d	4. e
2. b	5. c
3. a	

Exercise 2: Scene Two — Listening

1. go away
2. go swimming
3. took long walks
4. plenty of
5. wasn't crowded
6. what else
7. went dancing
8. went ice skating

Lesson 4

Listening Challenge

1. Wake up! You're late!
2. Don't fall asleep again! Get up!
3. Don't go back to sleep! Get out of bed!
4. Get dressed! You're late!
5. Put on a jacket! It's cold!
6. Have a nice day!

Exercise 1: Mini-Dialogues

1. d	5. b
2. g	6. f
3. e	7. a
4. c	

Exercise 2: Scene Two

1. get up
2. went back to sleep
3. had time
4. put on
5. took a shower
6. got dressed
7. need to

Lesson 5

Listening Challenge

1. b   4. c
2. c   5. b
3. a

Exercise 1: Mini-Dialogues

1.   **2.**

1. b   1. e
2. e   2. a
3. a   3. b
4. c   4. c
5. d   5. d

Exercise 2: Scene Two

1. Can I take your order
2. whatever you want
3. am very hungry
4. I'd like
5. I'll have
6. We're ready to order
7. What would you like
8. I'll have
9. how about you
10. Will that be all
11. for now

Lesson 6

Listening Challenge

1. take aspirin
2. drink tea
3. go to the dentist
4. do back exercises
5. go to the doctor

Exercise 1: Mini-Dialogues

1.   **2.**

1. e   1. a
2. a   2. d
3. d   3. c
4. b   4. b
5. c   5. e

Exercise 2: Scene Two

1. is killing me
2. What happened
3. fell down
4. is swollen
5. right away
6. I'll be right back
7. I think so

Lesson 7

Listening Challenge

1. it
2. them
3. it
4. it
5. them

Exercise 1: Mini-Dialogues

1. g   5. b
2. c   6. a
3. d   7. f
4. e   8. h

Exercise 2: Scene Two

1. we're just looking
2. Let me know
3. What do you think of
4. How much is it
5. try this on
6. over there
7. go on in
8. How does this look
9. We'll take it

Lesson 8

Listening Challenge

No one is going to do the dishes.

No one is going to do the laundry.

Exercise 1: Mini-Dialogues

1. d   5. c
2. a   6. g
3. f   7. h
4. b   8. e

Exercise 2: Scene Two

1. I'm lucky
2. did the laundry
3. the dishes
4. No problem
5. get home
6. can't wait
7. I'm getting sleepy
8. take a nap

Info Gaps

Lesson 3

FOR SPEAKER 1

(1) Here is information about YOUR summer. You will give this information to Speaker 2 when she/he asks you questions. You will sometimes need to add the words *Yes* and *No*.

My summer was great.	I played soccer.
I went away for two weeks.	I read two books.
I stayed with cousins.	Sometimes I took long walks on
I had a great time.	the beach.
I went swimming.	

(2) After you finish giving information about your summer to Speaker 2, ask him/her the following questions and fill out this chart. Just write short notes on the right. Don't try to write every word that Speaker 2 says.

Questions to ask Speaker 2:   Information from Speaker 2:

- How was your summer?

  _____

- Did you go away?

  _____

- What did you do on weekends?

  _____

- Did you have a good time?

  _____

- What else did you do?

  _____

- Do you want to go away next summer?

  _____

- Why?

  _____

Lesson 3

FOR SPEAKER 2

(1) Ask Speaker 1 the following questions and fill out this chart. Just write short notes on the right. Don't try to write every word that Speaker 1 says.

Questions to ask Speaker 1:

Information from Speaker 1:

- How was your summer?

_____

- Did you go away?

_____

- Did you stay in a hotel?

_____

- Who did you stay with?

_____

- Did you have a good time?

_____

- What did you do?

_____

- What else did you do?

_____

(2) Here is information about YOUR summer. You will give this information to Speaker 1 when she/he asks you questions. You will sometimes need to add the words *Yes* and *No.*

My summer was pretty good.

I didn't go away. I stayed home because I had to work.

On weekends, I often went to the beach with my family.

We had a great time.

We had barbecues and sometimes we rented videotapes.

I'm happy to stay home.

There are plenty of things to do at home, so I don't need to go away.

Lesson 7

FOR SPEAKER 1 (Seller)

You like selling old things at a flea market every weekend. Here is information about what you are selling. You will give this information to Speaker 2 when she or he asks you questions. If the shopper thinks your prices are too high (expensive), then you can "bargain." Sometimes you can sell something for a lower price, and sometimes you will not change your price. You decide.

Example of a conversation:

SHOPPER: How much do you want for these plates?

SELLER: They are $10 each. They are very old.

SHOPPER: Will you take $8? (Or: How about $8?)

Before you start, write the name of each item on small pieces of paper or 3" x 5" cards. On the back of the cards, write your prices. Put these cards on your desk so the shopper can see the items, but not the prices.

Items	Prices You Want to Get
very old plates	$10 each
a lamp	$25
a wooden table	$35
a beautiful pitcher	$15
a silver picture frame	$12
sunglasses	$10
_____	_____

When you finish, give the shopper what she or he bought (give the cards).

Lesson 7

FOR SPEAKER 2 (Shopper)

You just moved into a new apartment and you need many things. You are shopping at a flea market because you can find many interesting and unusual t hings there, and the prices are cheaper than in a department store.

One seller has many old and beautiful things to sell. You ask, "How much is this?" or "How much are these?" (Or: "How much do you want for this/these?") When she or he tells you the price, you can say, "That is too expensive" and then you can ask, "Will you take $___?" or "How about $___?" In other words, you can "bargain." But if you really want something, you can pay what the seller wants.

Example of a conversation:

SHOPPER: How much do you want for these plates?

SELLER: They are $10 each. They are very old.

SHOPPER: Will you take $8? (Or: How about $8?)

Here is a list of things the seller is trying to sell at the flea market:

Items	Prices You Can Pay
very old plates	$5 each
a lamp	$15
a wooden table	$28
a beautiful pitcher	$9
a silver picture frame	$7
sunglasses	$5
_____	_____

When you finish, take what you bought (the cards) and thank the seller.

Index: Alphabetical List of Expressions

(The numbers refer to the lesson numbers in this book.)